THE ROOM-BY-ROOM BOOK OF
AMERICAN ANTIQUES

THE BLACK-AND-WHITE
BOOK OF
AMERICAN
ANTIQUES

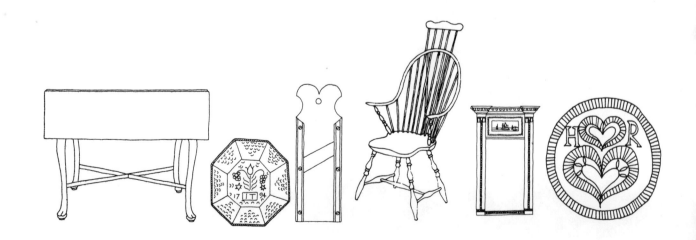

THE ROOM-BY-ROOM BOOK OF

AMERICAN ANTIQUES

BY

Cynthia & Julian Rockmore

GALAHAD BOOKS • NEW YORK CITY

Library of Congress Catalog Card Number: 75-12264
ISBN 0-88365-319-2
Printed in the United States of America
Published by arrangement with Hawthorn Books, Inc.

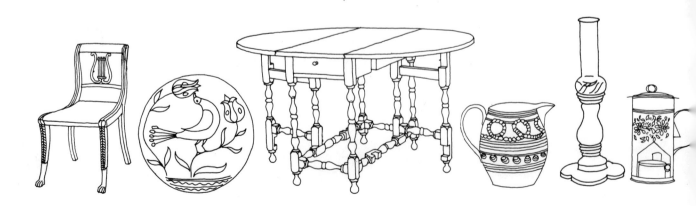

PREFACE

Customarily, a book is dedicated by the author to persons near and dear, or to those who helped in research or assisted with the reference material relative to the text, or to just plain Mom, who believed and encouraged.

We do not wish to appear sentimental nor do we want to drop names that might give important credence to our ideas, though perhaps we should, for there are many outstanding collectors, museum curators, and their benefactors who have had a most important effect on our opinions. But because this a book for the average American, we would like to dedicate it to those whose involvement with antiques is, as it has been through our entire lives, an everyday matter: the dealers, retailers, buyers for collections, decorators, auctioneers, cabinetmakers, and refinishers. These are the people who taught us about antiques. The Wonseys, Mr. Fry, and dear, departed Mrs. Burnham, of Central New England, who were the first to acquaint us with early handmade houses filled with early handmade furnishings; Amos Alexander, who lived in a house in Kelton Hill, Massachusetts, built by his great-great-granddad at a time when Indians roamed that area; Ralph Zettlemoyer, Warren Spirat, and Harry Hacker, all of Berks County, Pennsylvania, who helped us learn what they had spent a lifetime learning.

INTRODUCTION

A room is an unobstructed space appropriate for occupancy.

A room is also where all the "living with" starts. It is the area in which one must ultimately place those objects he has accumulated and with which he wishes to continue to surround himself.

If someone were to fill a room with Toby jugs, you might call it decorating with antiques. But you really would have to be a dedicated Toby-jug collector to have all those little round faces leering at you from all corners of a room.

The fixed area you live in and furnish should have a balance of interests for you. Unless you intend to be a hermit or you just don't care, a room should be pleasant to everyone who enters. Ideally, a room should be furnished to suit one's needs, interests, and comfort. Remember that comfort is both mental and physical, and the visual effect of the furnishings in a room has as great an effect on one's comfort as an abundance of overstuffed sofas.

We believe antiques are for everyone, simply because it is true. Everything we see or do pertaining to antiques reaffirms our belief that the well-designed functional and decorative objects of fine workmanship made today can be, if they survive, the antiques of the future.

There are many good reasons for making a study of any works of distinction. This is especially true for Americans who are interested in Americana, for it is a part of what we are. No matter how brief the

study, it is especially interesting to learn more about the early Colonies. If you are interested enough to collect the objects of those times, it will be doubly gratifying to know something of the people who made the objects you are now living with.

To learn about these impressive people who worked with basic materials and with primitive tools, the men and women who worked in wood, iron, glass, silver, and thread, and who made objects of great and lasting beauty, is to know about the artistic roots of this country.

It is important to know something of why and how these pieces were made. In many cases they were essential to the needs of survival in those perilous times. The simplicity and forthrightness of their construction is the result of the deep interest of the artisan who made them and shows his dedication to his work. Fine design and decorative qualities, outlets for the instinctive taste and feeling that the artisan had for color, symmetry, and texture, are to be seen in every piece that has endured all this time.

The very workmanship that has made these objects of so long ago last all these years commands the respect of the onlooker or collector. Because of this heritage, each of these articles, some in great collections and many more still moving from collector to dealer and dealer to collector, will continue to have an ever-increasing importance to Americans. Added to that, the enjoyment one derives just in possessing

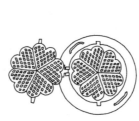

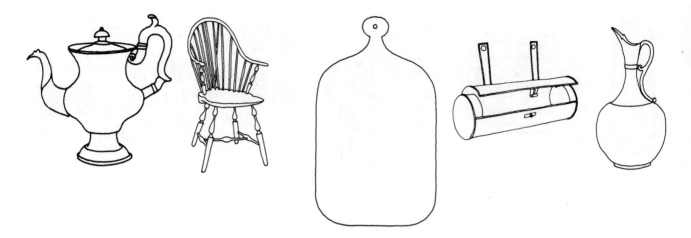

something of the early beginnings of this country makes these antiques rewarding and valuable indeed.

In its early years of development, this country moved so rapidly into the machine age that the quantity of very early antiques is limited. Even if we were to include antiques up to the end of the nineteenth century, we still could total only about three hundred years of working time, a very little time for a very few artisans to compete quantitatively with their European counterparts. It is no wonder that American antiques have such acceptability and ever-increasing value. In our populous country of some two hundred million Americans there is a constantly expanding market for these articles, utilitarian or purely decorative, representative of our roots.

Practically all Early American (primitive) man-made objects were utilitarian. The early settlers had little or no time for decorating. The makers of useful objects (blacksmiths, glassblowers, woodworkers, stonecutters, silversmiths) were specialists, so the articles they made took on the kind of functional beauty that comes from a worker who knows and likes what he is doing.

It may be immodest of us to liken ourselves to these early makers of lasting objects. It is only the fact that we, too, have spent a lifetime of involvement with this subject and have worked long and hard on the restoration of some of these pieces that, in a way, makes our attitude excusable.

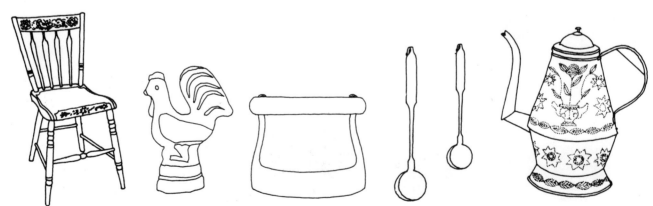

It was important to us to learn the meaning of these objects and to feel the dedication of the persons who made them. We have accomplished this, not simply as students, certainly not as armchair authors or purchasing agents motivated by trade, but as artists with respect and admiration for the work of the artisan.

Perhaps it would be valuable to tell you a bit about ourselves and why we feel this way.

We both are artists, educated and trained in art for our individual careers. We both have applied this art training over a long and successful period of time in the publication and advertising fields. We are both easel painters and enjoy the modest success of an occasional purchase and exhibiting in jury shows.

We have directed this professional background in art to the subject of this book, for we find antiques today uniquely interesting, entertaining, and important. And lastly, it is a subject that we have been deeply involved with for many years.

We know the feel of wood, stone, metal, and glass, for we have refinished them and polished them and handled them with loving care. We have moved them, turned them, lighted them to suit our way of viewing, and enjoyed them. These are some of the reasons that objects made of these materials and belonging to America's formative years have a deep and lived-with meaning for both of us.

It has often been said that the American dream is to discover an old, dilapidated, inexpensive, somewhere-in-the-country property and convert it into a home of beauty, comfort, and value. If one accomplishes this just once in a lifetime, and many couples have, it is considered quite an achievement.

Our first American dream came true by determination, prodigious physical effort, years of time, and judicious expenditure of limited amounts of cash. We went on to accomplish this same feat three additional times. It is because of our experiences in this restoration work that we became knowledgeable about the subject of antiques. And it was in these cumulative experiences that we were continuously exposed to almost all facets of antiquing. It was these labors of love in New England, Pennsylvania, and New Jersey that made us feel we were a part of that world of artisans, not just purchasers of pieces from it.

The years following art school gave us our start. There was time, things were cheap, and we were full of energy.

A bedraggled 1760 Cape Cod house in Massachusetts, a potential beauty in our eyes, but just a red blob on the local mortgage bank's books, set us off and restoring—knowing absolutely nothing of the things that would put a house together and fill it with the objects that make it look right—and make it look good. But we learned. The feel and finish of old wood, the modest shine of forged metal, the reserved color of pottery glazes, and the use of bright glass were where the decorating fun was for us. Most of the furnishings were purchased

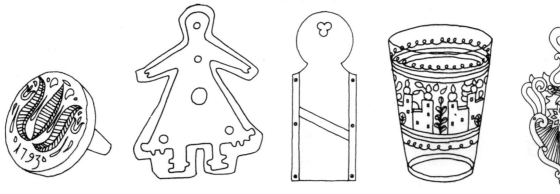

 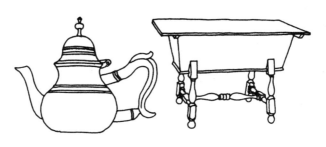 

in junk shops, secondhand stores, backwoods country auctions, and other places a couple, short of cash but long on ideas, would shop. Refinishing and rebuilding were part of almost every purchase.

Of course, there were books on the subject. But they dealt mainly with the same unobtainable museum and private collection pieces that many new books still treat. These objects of Americana would be difficult to purchase even with unlimited amounts of money. Obviously, we had to content ourselves with the antiques that were available and within our meager means. Later we spent time learning about the more precious pieces as we found them and could afford to own them.

Our interest in the stone houses of the Pennsylvania Dutch country led us to Berks County. The move was predicated by our need to be closer to New York City, where we worked, and our continuing desire for a place in the country. Curiosity concerning the Pennsylvania Dutch and the almost indestructible construction of their houses brought us to our second mammoth undertaking.

The contrast beween these two peoples, the New Englanders and the Pennsylvania Dutch, who settled in this new world at approximately the same time and for many of the same reasons, was fascinating. But the almost endless source of primitive and Victorian antiques was, to us, simply irresistible, and made our moving to that area even more desirable.

This second restoration project was an 1803 double stone house in Mill Creek, Berks County, Pennsylvania. Anyone attempting to restore a second early house, after just having completed renovating one, has got to be odd. And if you add to that the impossible problems to be found in a stone house with twenty-six-inch-thick walls, you know that the renovators must, at the very least, be testing themselves.

When this labor of love was completed, and taken off our hands by an interested and financially-able couple, we directed our time, talent, money, and muscle to the rehabilitation of our third dream house, a William Penn grant property with a dilapidated 1752 stone house on a hilltop in Kempton, Pennsylvania, ten miles to the north of Mill Creek.

With the lessons in restoration having been well learned and still fresh in our minds and calluses, we were able to complete the reconstruction of the Kempton house and to enjoy decorating it with the best of our then-abundant collection of antiques.

Our fourth and last renovation was an unimpressive, well-beaten 140-year-old farmhouse in Mountainside, New Jersey. This was important, for we now had to have a home within commuting distance of our New York jobs.

To read this resumé of our antiques past, one might assume this book would be a treatise on how to buy an old broken-down house and make it a property of beauty and value. Indeed, that may be a book of ours for the future.

But this rather detailed review of the past is only to prove to the reader that armchair experts we aren't. We have learned about antiques by knowing what they are, first, and what their names are, second. Their texture, design, color, and decorative possibilities are part of our artistic upbringing, and we hope we will be able to impart some of this interest, information, and excitement to you, our readers.

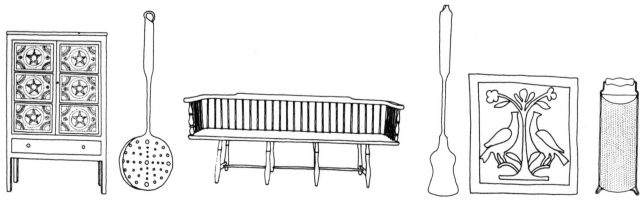

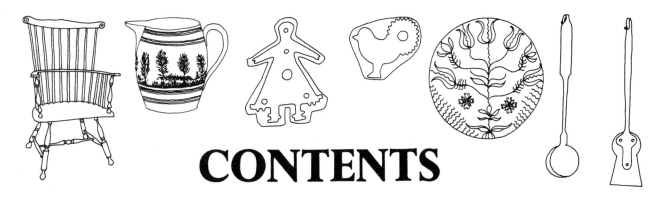

CONTENTS

In order to cover the whole subject of American antiques, we decided to separate the chapters in this book room by room, for that is the way people live.

There surely is enough antiques material to fill a book about each room in the house. Nevertheless, we have chosen to write about and illustrate seven separate living areas in this book, and to place the antiques shown in the areas we believe appropriate for them. There is bound to be some crossover, for some of the more primitive antiques date from a period when an entire family lived in one room. We have, therefore, taken the artistic prerogative of placing these antiques in a room and in a way that we believe they could be comfortably lived with now.

Furnishings shown in the color section are from the authors' collection unless otherwise specified. Photographs by Don Piper.

Duncan Phyfe carved mahogany sofa. Two rosettes terminate the foot scrolls. Rosettes and prominent reeded motif are an integral part of the back design. 1815.

THE LIVING ROOM

When couples start to furnish a home for themselves, it is normal for them to begin with the things that perform those functions essential to their everyday living. They have little thought—and little money—for objects that are purely decorative. Utilitarian furnishings with the best construction and design that their funds can provide are what they generally seek. Ordinarily, this is deemed a practical procedure for furnishing a new home, particularly at today's prices.

If we take exception to this time-honored practice, it is only in an attempt to improve the long-term result. We would like to help them avoid making the same errors a good proportion of the young couples that preceded them made a generation before, for after they live with furnishings that are dated and drab long before the time payments are completed, they will have realized that better things would have been more sensible. Now we must remind you that better things does not necessarily mean more expensive

things. What it does mean is better-thought-out things.

A nineteenth-century decorative iron bed, constructed specifically to hold a full-size mattress and spring, can still be purchased for only a few dollars. It will be considerably less than the cost of the factory-manufactured, veneered-wood, simulated-finished furnishings of these times, furniture that has no charm and is very likely to have less as time and usage steadily decrease its monetary value.

Now, we are not suggesting you buy an antique car, although it might be a good investment. But furnishings have few running parts and, if carefully chosen, they will last almost forever. We are also not suggesting that you buy a nineteenth-century decorative iron bed, even when they are still purchasable for little money, unless you find one that is both attractive and practical.

What we are really telling you is to look about you and see the necessity of making your home an interesting, attractive,

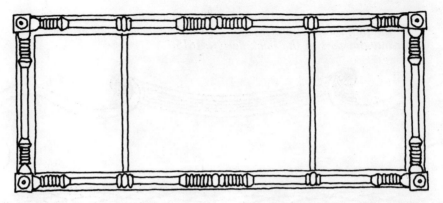

and comfortable place in which to spend your leisure time. Then give it the personality you wish it to have, for it is important to you and your family. Make it a place your children will enjoy living in, for the things that furnish it should be

meaningful enough to give your young ones pleasant roots and memories.

Mixing and matching periods of American antiques creates a dimension that is rarely, if ever, written about in books on this subject. It demonstrates one of the

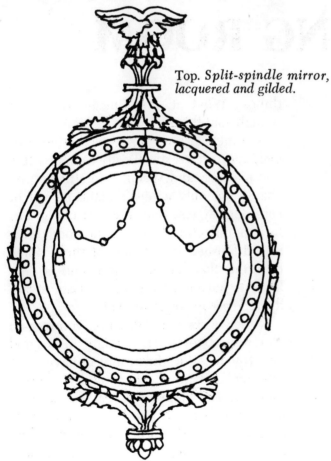

Top. *Split-spindle mirror, lacquered and gilded.*

Above. *Regency carved and gilded girandole mirror with side candle brackets is crowned with an eagle. An English import, it dates from around 1815.*

Right. *Federal carved and gilded mirror with panel depicts George Washington's monument.*

Above. A medallion-back sofa of walnut, a middle-1800's piece, is made into a comfortable settee. The Civil War–period mable-top table has been cut down to usable height. The half-spindle gilded mirror has a colorful Pennsylvania Dutch primitive painting in its top panel. The hanging lamp with a brass ball counterweight on a solid rod is an interesting bit of Victorian engineering.

Upper right. Typical Pennsylvania-Dutch pie safe. The lamp and cheese scale are from New England and are late Victorian.

Right. Open cupboards of this early Pennsylvania type are inclined to be catchalls for collectors. The rattail hinges on the panel doors of the base and the basic design date the base as very early eighteenth century. The top appears to have had some repair. The bric-a-brac on the shelves is ironstone, Leeds, Chelsea, pressed glass, and carnival glass. The baskets on top are all beaten ash and are typically early Pennsylvania Dutch. The Bennington crock in the lower corner has an unusual decoration in cobalt glaze.

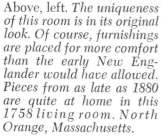

Above, left. *The uniqueness of this room is in its original look. Of course, furnishings are placed for more comfort than the early New Englander would have allowed. Pieces from as late as 1880 are quite at home in this 1758 living room. North Orange, Massachusetts.*

Far left. *Philadelphia Queen Anne chair, 1780. The original fabric is all needlepoint with center design in petit point.* (Edwin F. Nimmo Collection, Barto, Pennsylvania)

Left. *An Adams mantelpiece from an early Connecticut house holds two early pewter teapots of classic design. The unusual three-piece-mold milk-glass vases are Victorian. The sconces are ormolu. The wall pieces show the French influence on these early brass castings. The cast-iron match holder is from New England.*

Above. *The corner of this living room shows an interesting mixture of periods: A very early burl bowl lives happily with a late milk-glass piece. The compote from Ephrata, Pennsylvania, is of two-piece-mold pressed-glass—mid-1800's. The early Victorian hanging lamp has a rare shade of hobnail Vaseline glass. The cherry corner cupboard contains patterned ironstone and saw-tooth pressed-glass pieces. The blown decanters on the top shelf are very early. The mahogany tilt-top table is an early Pennsylvania piece.*

Right. *The small fireplace in this early house in the Pennsylvania-Dutch country is an example of the chair rail connecting with everything wood. The brass clock is a commemorative casting from the late 1800's. The Chelsea sugar bowl makes an attractive flower vase. The early Windsor rocker is from New England; the maple oval tilt-top table is Victorian.*

Below. *A late Victorian wall clock over a primitive Windsor and an early New England maple candlestand alongside a late Victorian gentleman's chair all make a rather comfortable grouping. The cat seems to approve. The Georgian brass candlestick with pressed-glass girandoles adds a bright touch, as does the bracket lamp between the windows.*

Below. *A marble-top commode feels comfortable next to a rosewood lady's chair. They and the brass lamp are all of about the same late Victorian period. The cranberry-glass thumbprint shade on the wall bracket is perhaps a bit earlier.*

interesting effects that collecting and decorating has on the children of the house. In years back, when decorating a room for a child was a sentimental spree for the parents and as backward as baby talk, children had little voice in the choice of decoration in their quarters, and certainly none in the decor of the rest of the house. A child's interest in the beauty of his home has a profound effect on his present and future desires. It is certainly important to think about the fact that children love color, objects of other times and places, items with history, filled with the romance of lives that preceded theirs. Names, dates, makers, and cost have little significance in their interest in anything they are drawn toward.

Upper right. *Empire mirror with landscape painting on underside of glass.*

Center. *Georgian carved and gilded mahogany architectural mirror. Eighteenth century.*

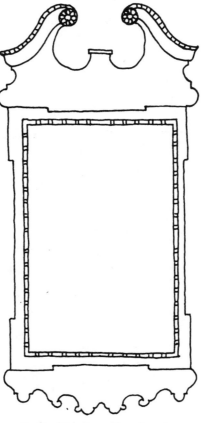

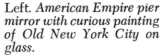

Left. *American Empire pier mirror with curious painting of Old New York City on glass.*

Right. *Mirror with landscape painted on the reverse side of glass. About 1840.* (Landis Valley Museum)

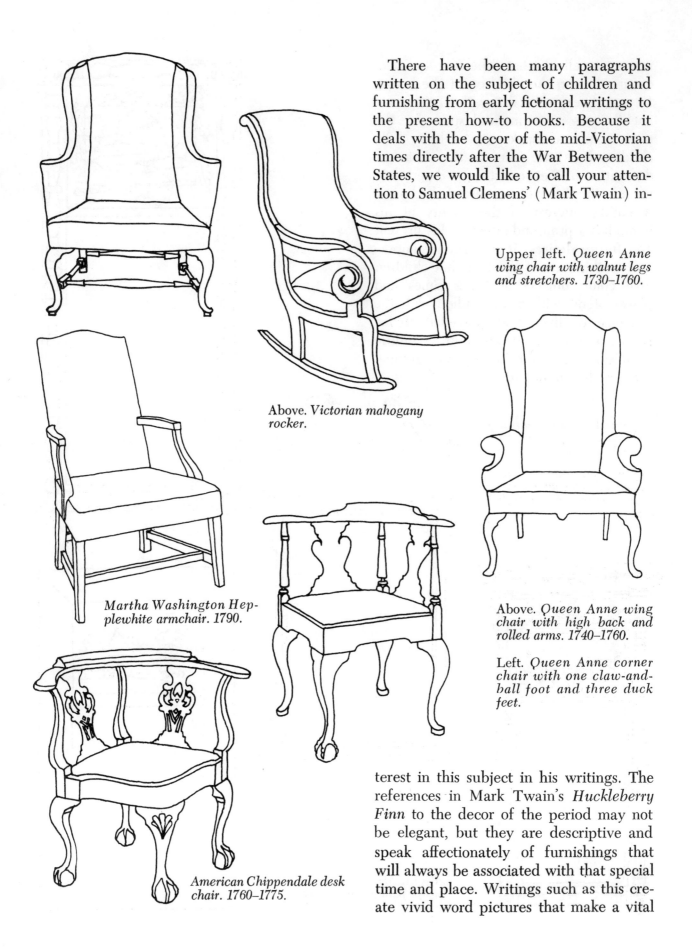

There have been many paragraphs written on the subject of children and furnishing from early fictional writings to the present how-to books. Because it deals with the decor of the mid-Victorian times directly after the War Between the States, we would like to call your attention to Samuel Clemens' (Mark Twain) in-

Upper left. *Queen Anne wing chair with walnut legs and stretchers. 1730–1760.*

Above. *Victorian mahogany rocker.*

Martha Washington Hepplewhite armchair. 1790.

Above. *Queen Anne wing chair with high back and rolled arms. 1740–1760.*

Left. *Queen Anne corner chair with one claw-and-ball foot and three duck feet.*

American Chippendale desk chair. 1760–1775.

terest in this subject in his writings. The references in Mark Twain's *Huckleberry Finn* to the decor of the period may not be elegant, but they are descriptive and speak affectionately of furnishings that will always be associated with that special time and place. Writings such as this create vivid word pictures that make a vital contribution to our understanding of specific periods in our history. The quote comes from the chapter entitled "The Grangerfords Take Me In." Huckleberry Finn:

"It was a mighty nice family and a mighty nice house, too. I hadn't seen no house out in the country before that was so nice and had so much style. It didn't have an iron latch on the front door, nor a wooden one with a buckskin string, but a brass knob to turn, the same as houses in town. There weren't no bed in the parlor, but there was a big fireplace that was bricked on

Above. *Chippendale secretary cabinet.*

Above. *Mahogany pie-crust table of Philadelphia origin. 1750–1775.*

Right. *Chippendale wing chair with mahogany stretchers. 1750–1775.*

Lower right. *Small pine side table with stretchers. Early 1700's.* (Metropolitan Museum)

Queen Anne highboy.

theirs, it will help you both learn something of the past and future of collecting and decorating while you are enjoying your surroundings of the present together.

The subject of how Mod some antiques are now, and how some young people equate these furnishings of the past with their rather individual ideas of the present and future, is of course something else. It is a subject that has had an important impact on the prices of many late Victorian antiques and items of decor that

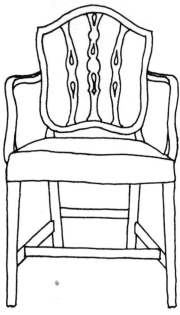

Hepplewhite armchair. 1790.

the bottom, and the bricks was kept clean and red by scrubbing them. They had big brass dog-irons that could hold up a saw log. And there was a clock on the mantelpiece with a picture of a town painted on the bottom half of the glass front.

"On the table in the middle of the room was a kind of lovely crockery basket that had apples and oranges and peaches and grapes piled up in it which was much redder and yellower and prettier than real ones is."

We suggest that when your children approve of your decor, as you should of

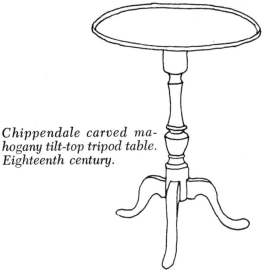

Chippendale carved mahogany tilt-top tripod table. Eighteenth century.

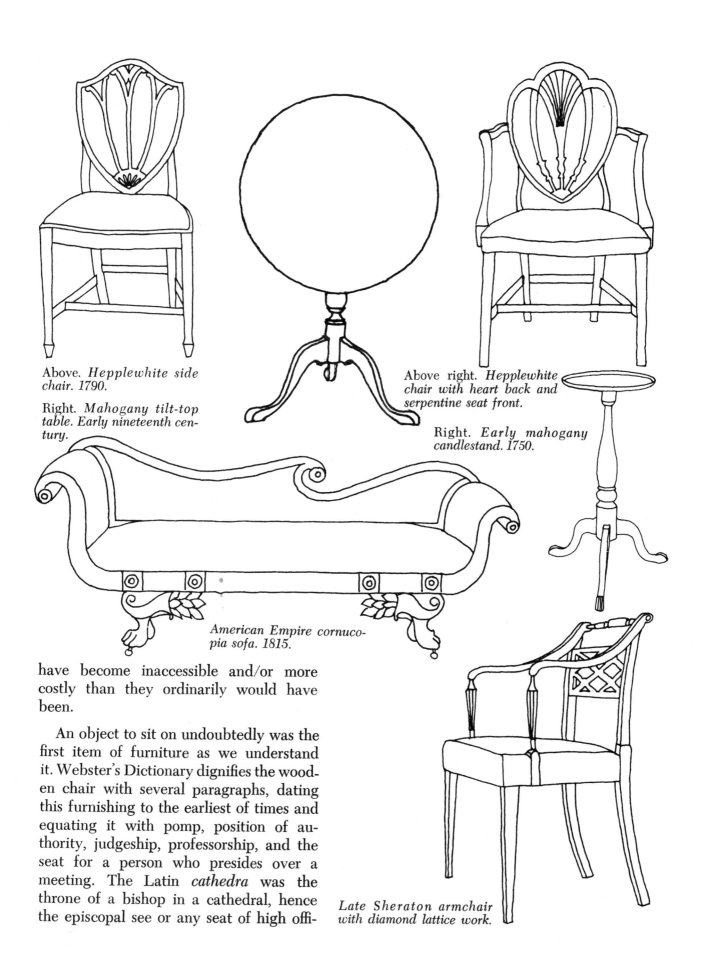

Above. *Hepplewhite side chair. 1790.*

Right. *Mahogany tilt-top table. Early nineteenth century.*

Above right. *Hepplewhite chair with heart back and serpentine seat front.*

Right. *Early mahogany candlestand. 1750.*

American Empire cornucopia sofa. 1815.

have become inaccessible and/or more costly than they ordinarily would have been.

An object to sit on undoubtedly was the first item of furniture as we understand it. Webster's Dictionary dignifies the wooden chair with several paragraphs, dating this furnishing to the earliest of times and equating it with pomp, position of authority, judgeship, professorship, and the seat for a person who presides over a meeting. The Latin *cathedra* was the throne of a bishop in a cathedral, hence the episcopal see or any seat of high offi-

Late Sheraton armchair with diamond lattice work.

cial authority. So the next time you sit down, think about it. Chair forms are legion and every cabinetmaker of every period of history designed and made quantities of them. American cabinetmakers were no exception.

However your living room is furnished, you probably own a greater variety of chairs than of any other individual category of your furnishings. The basic styles of American chair makers are not difficult to identify in their pure form. It is in the variations of those basic designs that it is easy to become confused. We have tried to show some of these variations in our illustrations, for we believe that visual reference is the only way to understand the makers' variations of their own designs.

The English Jacobean style is very familiar to Americans. These solid, simple, and heavy furnishings still exist now in reasonable quantity, undoubtedly because of their indestructible construction—they surely could not have been cherished because of their comfort. Though the Jacobean style (1600–1650) predated colonial times, it did exert considerable influence on American cabinetmakers then and still

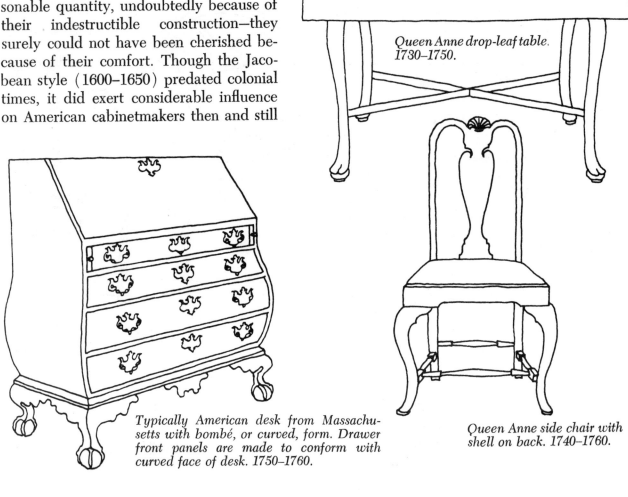

Right. *Philadelphia Queen Anne armchair. 1730–1750*

Candlestand. 1780

Queen Anne drop-leaf table. 1730–1750.

Typically American desk from Massachusetts with bombé, or curved, form. Drawer front panels are made to conform with curved face of desk. 1750–1760.

Queen Anne side chair with shell on back. 1740–1760.

does. The later and more sophisticated Restoration period, with its spiral turnings, stretcher bases, and a touch of influence from the Flemish cabinetmakers, gained in popularity in the Colonies right up until the eighteenth century. The great quantities of walnut and oak available in all the northern Colonies made this style of furnishing simple to make from the standpoint of fine raw material. The solid feel and look of the William and Mary pieces of about the same period were well suited to the practical need for sturdy seating. It was not until the attractive Queen Anne style, immediately followed by the Early Georgian style, that comfort, grace, and delicate beauty were added to the utilitarian values of the earlier styles of chairs and benches.

During the last quarter of the eighteenth century the better known cabinetmakers began making the pieces now so valuable and sought after by American collectors. Chippendale, with his interest in experimenting with a great variety of styles, was one of these early prominent makers (1740). His work was influenced

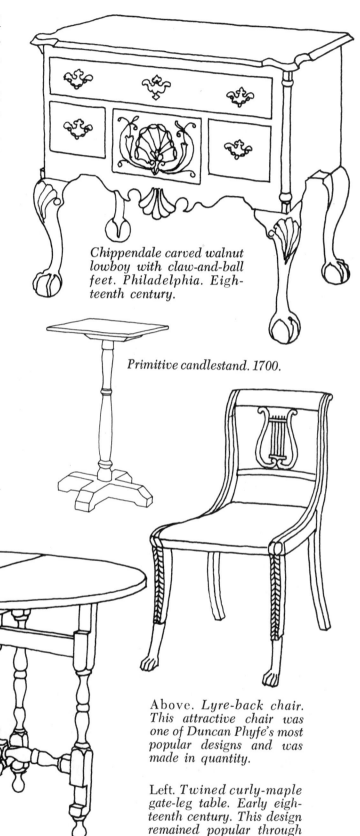

Chippendale carved walnut lowboy with claw-and-ball feet. Philadelphia. Eighteenth century.

Primitive candlestand. 1700.

Above. *Lyre-back chair. This attractive chair was one of Duncan Phyfe's most popular designs and was made in quantity.*

Left. *Twined curly-maple gate-leg table. Early eighteenth century. This design remained popular through the nineteenth century.*

Right. *Chest-on-chest. New England.*

Below. *Hepplewhite tilt-top table with spade feet. 1790.*

Below. *Small Queen Anne cherry tilt-top table. 1750.*

by the French makers whose designs at that time were following the fashionable trend in chinoiserie then so popular in Western Europe. Adam, a Scotsman of the same period, was also a maker of furnishings of fine quality and had been strongly influenced by classic Greek and ancient Italian motifs. His works became a tremendous and lasting influence in cabinet and mantel design, right up until the end of the eighteenth century.

The more delicate and familiar forms of Hepplewhite and Sheraton bring us into the early nineteenth century. The dark woods and ormolu of the French and Empire periods of the Regency style had great appeal to the more well-to-do Americans, who could now afford both comfort and style, and who relished the appearance of this ornate luxury so reminiscent to them of European royalty. Napoleon was the news of that time and many of the Empire furnishings show the interest and influence he exerted.

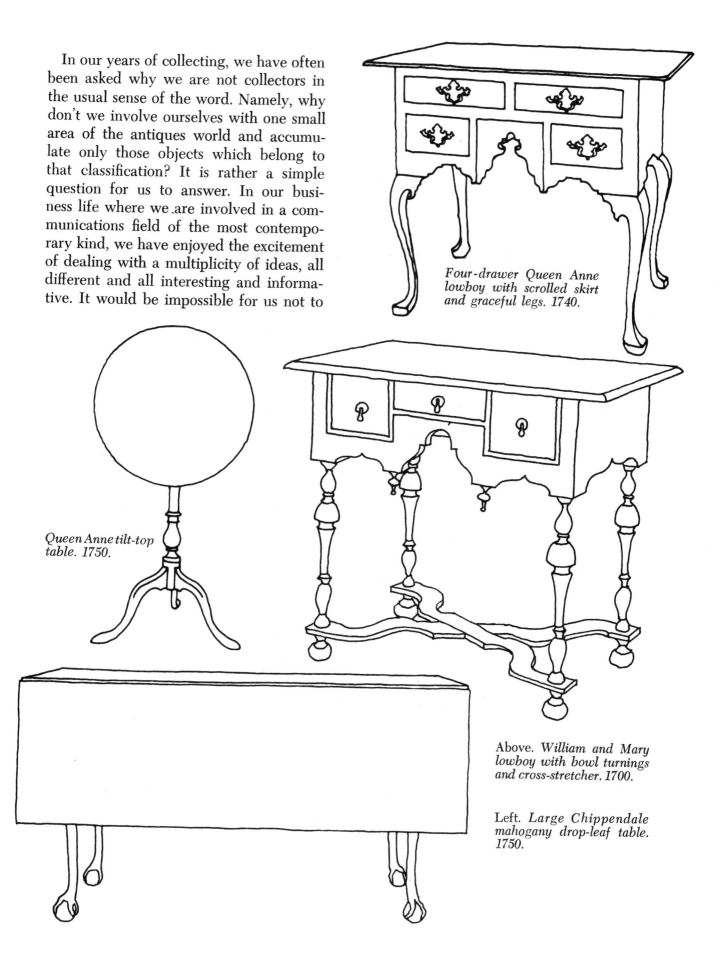

In our years of collecting, we have often been asked why we are not collectors in the usual sense of the word. Namely, why don't we involve ourselves with one small area of the antiques world and accumulate only those objects which belong to that classification? It is rather a simple question for us to answer. In our business life where we are involved in a communications field of the most contemporary kind, we have enjoyed the excitement of dealing with a multiplicity of ideas, all different and all interesting and informative. It would be impossible for us not to

Four-drawer Queen Anne lowboy with scrolled skirt and graceful legs. 1740.

Queen Anne tilt-top table. 1750.

Above. William and Mary lowboy with bowl turnings and cross-stretcher. 1700.

Left. Large Chippendale mahogany drop-leaf table. 1750.

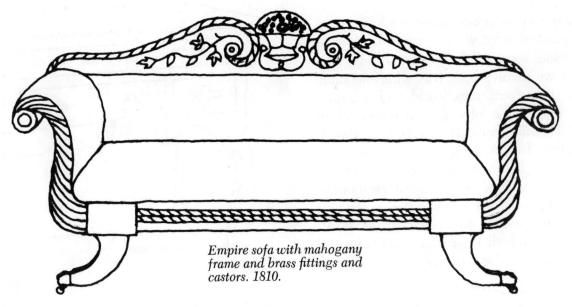

Empire sofa with mahogany frame and brass fittings and castors. 1810.

be interested in a subject, even if we know little about it. Instinctively, we try to learn all its ramifications simply because the learning entertains us so much. There is nothing wrong with dedicated collectors of a single category of any kind that inspires them. It is simply not the way we think. We do not collect to save or accumulate. We collect to live with. We find it most stimulating to surround ourselves with a variety of objects from all periods, and to be free to vary the arrangement of these objects in our home when and as we choose. If we have accumulated antiques as if we were squirrels preparing for winter, it is only because we delight in decorating with the antiques we like.

Everyone cannot have and may not want an old and traditional house. Yet many have a desire to collect American

Above. *Queen Anne rectangular tray-top table. 1730–1750.*

Right. *Queen Anne walnut tavern table. 1700's.*

Empire sofa with walnut frame and cast-brass feet. 1820.

antiques and have them play a part in their everyday living. With color, wallpaper and wall texture, and the careful choice and use of fabric, it is possible to simulate the feel of an early room yet still enjoy the most modern structural detail. We are not directing this book to purists, for that is a separate category of collecting. Indeed, nowadays for the purist to decorate with antiques would demand construction details and costs that would be astronomical if one did not already own an early house in very good repair.

Gilded eagle and cornucopia mirror has a circular frame with acorn ornaments and metal sconces for two candles. 1815.

Small Queen Anne sofa with shell carving, drake feet, gracefully scrolled back and rolled arm. 1750. (Metropolitan Museum)

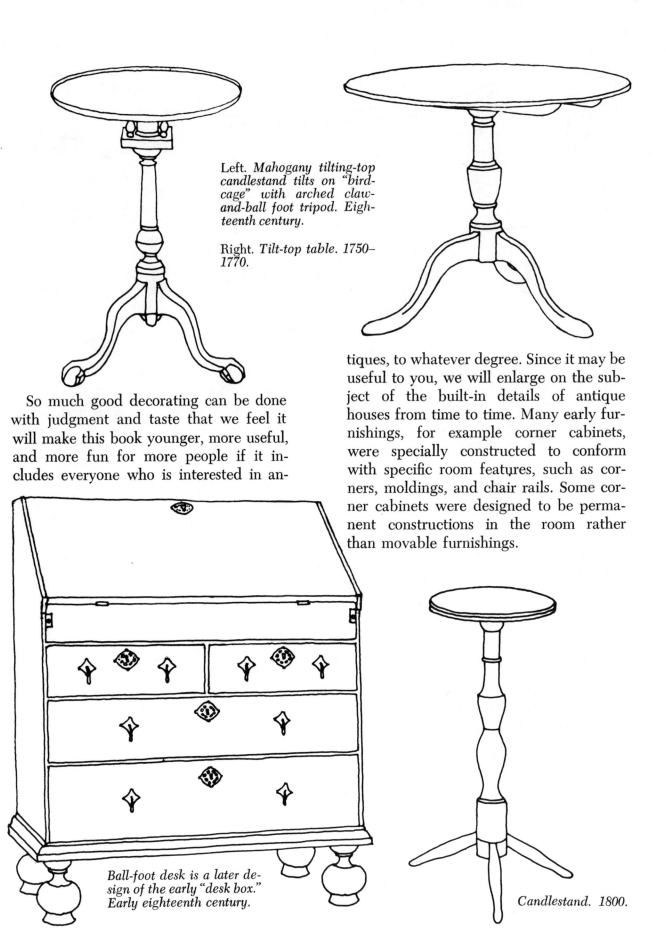

Left. *Mahogany tilting-top candlestand tilts on "birdcage" with arched claw-and-ball foot tripod. Eighteenth century.*

Right. *Tilt-top table. 1750–1770.*

tiques, to whatever degree. Since it may be useful to you, we will enlarge on the subject of the built-in details of antique houses from time to time. Many early furnishings, for example corner cabinets, were specially constructed to conform with specific room features, such as corners, moldings, and chair rails. Some corner cabinets were designed to be permanent constructions in the room rather than movable furnishings.

So much good decorating can be done with judgment and taste that we feel it will make this book younger, more useful, and more fun for more people if it includes everyone who is interested in an-

Ball-foot desk is a later design of the early "desk box." Early eighteenth century.

Candlestand. 1800.

The physical makeup of the rooms we live in are almost always an established fact before we start to impose our personalities upon them. If you are building your own home, of course, you will be imposing some of your functional and decorating ideas before you furnish any given area, for you know and feel how you want the total result to look when it is complete. This is a very special talent, for there are precious few people who can visualize completed and furnished homes from architectural plans. In any case, it is surprising and rewarding to see just what good ideas and ingenuity can do to change

Above. *Queen Anne high-boy.*

Left. *William and Mary six-legged highboy. New England. 1700.*

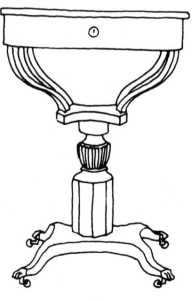

Empire work table. 1800–1810.

Below. *Pillar-and-scroll clock with eight-day brass movement. H. Clark, Plymouth, Connecticut. 1820.*

Left. *Grandmother clock, or dwarf tall clock. Massachusetts. 1780.*

Above. *Ogee clock with thirty-hour brass movement. 1838.*

Below. *Seth Thomas eight-day calendar clock. 1860.*

a room with homely basic construction. Therefore, it is sensible to think for a moment about those constructions and fixtures that will need to be camouflaged ingeniously to make them part of what you want the whole attitude of the room to be. There are various ways in which ceilings can be raised or lowered optically with the use of color. Windows can be made to appear larger with the positioning of draperies. Most doorways are not really doorways any more, but simply openings between one room and another. They perform the artistic function of a frame for the room beyond.

As you view a section of one room from another through the doorway frame, color can keep each adjoining room separate and at the same time harmoniously connected. Incidentally, if there is a door in the doorway (which is no longer a must),

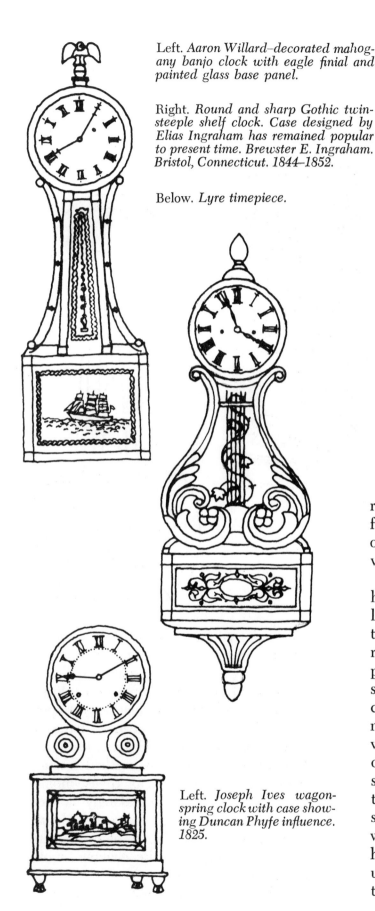

Left. Aaron Willard–decorated mahogany banjo clock with eagle finial and painted glass base panel.

Right. Round and sharp Gothic twin-steeple shelf clock. Case designed by Elias Ingraham has remained popular to present time. Brewster E. Ingraham. Bristol, Connecticut. 1844–1852.

Below. Lyre timepiece.

Left. Joseph Ives wagon-spring clock with case showing Duncan Phyfe influence. 1825.

remember that at least one of the two faces of that door must satisfy the decor of two rooms. Once again, color plays a very important role in this.

As the social gathering place in the house expanded from the kitchen to the living room, many changes in the decorative and functional details of these two rooms were affected. For instance, the fireplace became part of the living room. In some of the lesser details of decoration, changes also became apparent. In the most primitive kitchens, for example, the windows rarely had curtains. Indeed, some of the earliest kitchens had only homespun over the opening in the outside wall that was later to be windowed. But as small luxuries and time for decorating were made available to the woman of the house, cotton or homespun curtains were used to cover windows, including those of the kitchen. Moreover, the shift in living

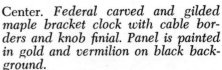

Center. *Federal carved and gilded maple bracket clock with cable borders and knob finial. Panel is painted in gold and vermilion on black background.*

Below. *Howard banjo clock. E. Howard & Company, Boston, Massachusetts.*

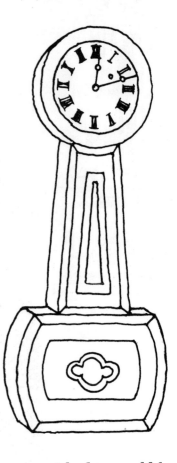

Above. *Steeple-on-steeple clock. Birge and Fuller, Bristol, Connecticut. 1845.*

Left. *Eight-day wood movement clock has decal work and painting on glass. Eli Terry and Sons.*

areas allowed for materials that would be suitable in a room separated from cooking, smoke, and odors. Living room windows could now be covered with colorful curtains and, later, with luxurious draperies of fine silks and brocades, materials much more attractive and much less practical than the ever-to-be-washed kitchen cousin. People also began to use homespun, braided, and painstakingly hooked rugs and runners which warmed the living room floors without worry of the hazard of food spillage and the cooking smoke and grease of the kitchen.

Wild flowers, at best not too hardy once

Below. Lighthouse clock. The base of the clock is built of pine and veneered with mahogany. Roxbury movement by Simon Willard. 1822.

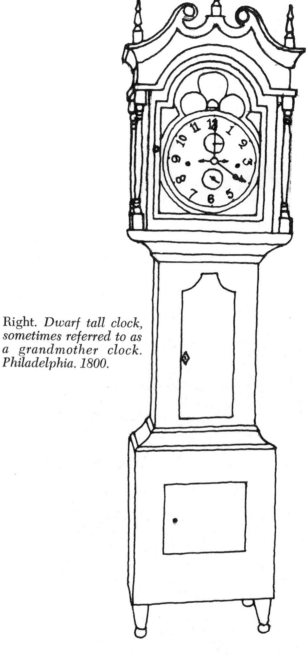

Right. Dwarf tall clock, sometimes referred to as a grandmother clock. Philadelphia. 1800.

picked, were found to keep much longer away from the kitchen stove. Dried grain and dried wild flower decorations remained clean even when not covered with a glass bell. The whole change to a separate living area favored the ever-present need of the woman of the house to accumulate pretty things as well as useful things, and to place them where they pleased her.

Colorful pieces of glass and pottery, and fancy needlework, then prints or clippings from early publications, and memorabilia of almost every description found themselves in permanent residence in the room. They were rarely, if ever, moved from their original places from one decade to another. In some homes, the parlor or living room was not even used as a

37

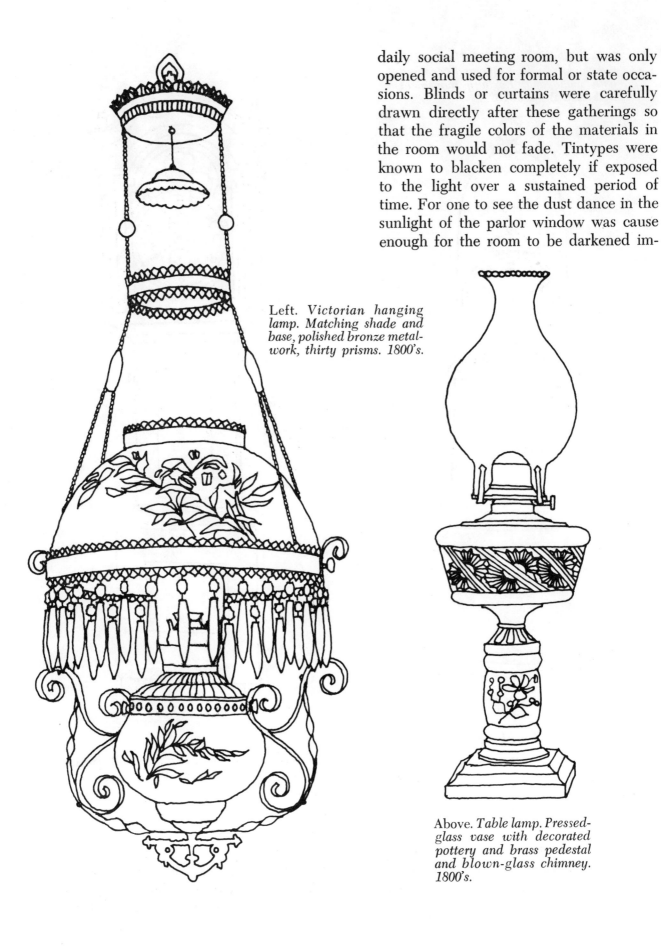

daily social meeting room, but was only opened and used for formal or state occasions. Blinds or curtains were carefully drawn directly after these gatherings so that the fragile colors of the materials in the room would not fade. Tintypes were known to blacken completely if exposed to the light over a sustained period of time. For one to see the dust dance in the sunlight of the parlor window was cause enough for the room to be darkened im-

Left. *Victorian hanging lamp. Matching shade and base, polished bronze metalwork, thirty prisms. 1800's.*

Above. *Table lamp. Pressed-glass vase with decorated pottery and brass pedestal and blown-glass chimney. 1800's.*

mediately; with the lack of light it seemed to the woman of the house that there was no longer any dust.

Of course, as bric-a-brac was accumulated by the family, objects were added to the parlor and were sometimes made a part of the permanent collection on the table or mantelpiece or whatnot shelves. Frequently the clutter became so unbearable that it was essential for the woman of the house finally and reluctantly to remove an occasional piece and store it in

the attic where it was bound to remain for generations.

All this collecting and placing on display was simply the beginning of decorating a home. It had little to do with living as we know it, for the idea of comfort and ease, so much a part of our time, was not a luxury to be dreamed of then. The objects that gave people of those times joy, fortunately, were very carefully kept; it is because of the care they gave them then that we can now collect and

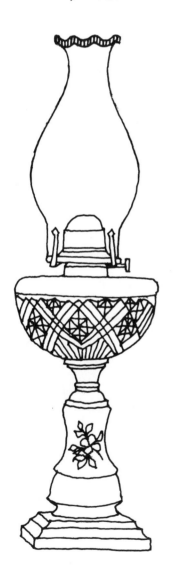

Below. *Table lamp with pressed-glass vase, pottery and iron pedestal.*

Above. *Table lamp with pressed-glass vase, decorated glass and brass base. 1800's.*

Below. *Table lamp with vase and pedestal of pressed glass, fine blown-glass chimney.*

enjoy the very same objects of beauty and antiquity.

But the preciousness of those days is inclined to hang on and, when it does, the fun of collecting and enjoying these items becomes stale, a thing of the past. The mere accumulation of memorabilia without discrimination is not collecting with any idea of decorating or comfort in mind. It is not hard to have a room look simply old-fashioned. Contemporary decorating with antiques presupposes the enjoyment of cherished objects of American antiquity in the mood and comfort of the present.

One would suppose the living room took over as the family gathering place simply because it was usually the largest room in the house. But, remember that at one time all living, sleeping, cooking and eating took place in one room. So it is difficult to determine whether the kitchen became separate from the living room or vice versa. Central heating certainly played a part in this change because it was then no longer necessary to be leg-length from the kitchen stove or fireplace to be warm.

Above and right. *Pewter lamps with one or two wicks. Early eighteenth century.*

Left. *Pressed-glass table lamp, pedestal of painted glass, brass fittings and base.*

Queen Anne tray-top table.

Most living rooms borrowed ideas from the kitchen—the fireplace, for instance, was first a necessity (heat) and second an attractive fixture. There were probably deep-rooted emotional reasons for the borrowing, too. It was also possible to add comfortable chairs, lamps, and tables to the larger area that the living room could offer and, as a natural consequence, there were now some unneeded surfaces that could be decorated with objects other than cooking utensils.

The fireplace developed a lower, wider mantelpiece and, in some cases, a decorative front. At times, the mantel of this period was covered with a popular material to conceal its basic construction. The hearth was furnished with firedogs or and-

Above. *One- and two-wick pewter lamps. Early eighteenth century.*

Right. *Pressed-glass table lamp with bronze fittings. Fount and base are of dark green glass; the base is painted. Eighteenth century.*

Above. *Brass whale-oil and camphene lamp. 1840.*

Right. *Pewter bull's-eye lamp. 1800's.*

irons of cast or wrought iron, or bright
brass tools for managing the fire were
placed along its side, and fire rails and a
screen covered its front face to catch flying sparks. It all tended to make the fireplace, that once almost entirely utilitarian
area, an ideal focal point of the living
room space.

The well-scrubbed brick floor of the
hearth, once covered with the ash of many
fires, was no longer dusty grey as a re-
minder of its essential and utilitarian past.

The transition of fireplaces to a new

*Three milk-glass smoke
bells.*

*Above. Heavy cast-iron bracket lamp
with pressed-glass fount and brass fittings was cast especially for Grange
Hall, Orange, Massachusetts. About
1843.*

and practical use is, in itself, a record of our early history. Fire-backs, covered with intricate decorations in bas relief, were cast in early colonial foundries. These heavy iron castings were placed in the back of fireplaces to retain the heat of the fire and thus to continue to warm the room long after the wood had burned out. They were the beginnings of the stove as we know it. The earliest examples of heating stoves used in the Pennsylvania country were five-sided, cast-iron boxes performing the function of stove and fire-

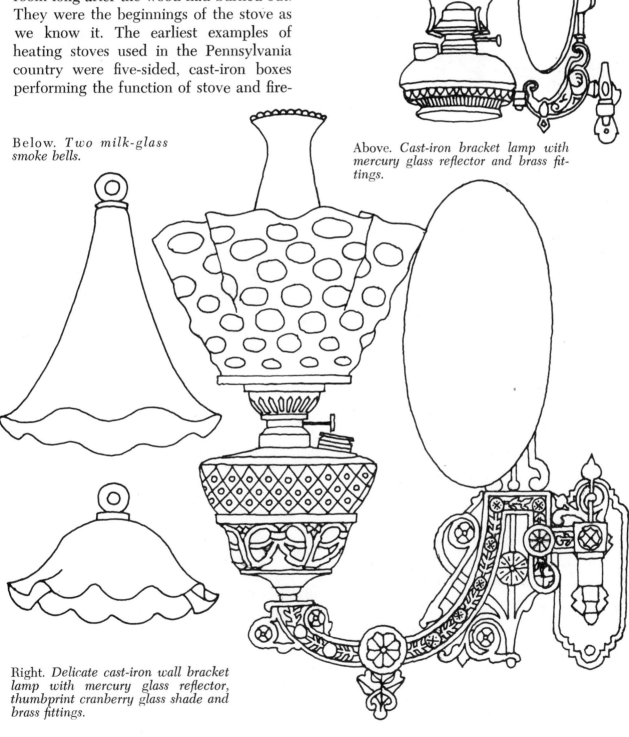

Above. *Cast-iron bracket lamp with mercury glass reflector and brass fittings.*

Below. *Two milk-glass smoke bells.*

Right. *Delicate cast-iron wall bracket lamp with mercury glass reflector, thumbprint cranberry glass shade and brass fittings.*

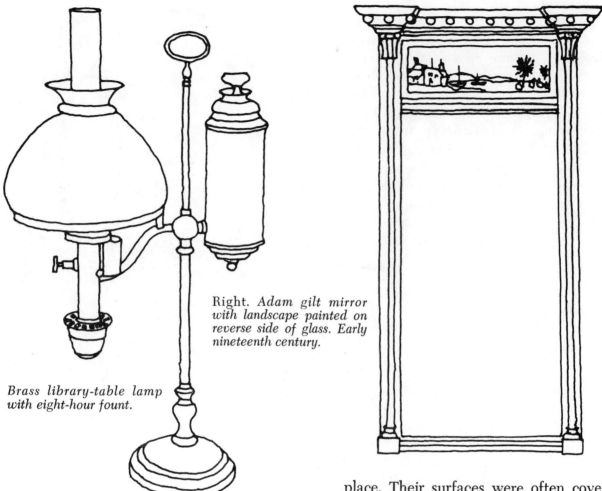

Right. *Adam gilt mirror with landscape painted on reverse side of glass. Early nineteenth century.*

Brass library-table lamp with eight-hour fount.

Below. *Chippendale side chair. 1740–1760.*

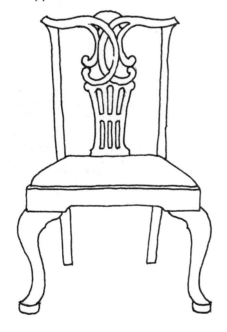

place. Their surfaces were often covered with bas relief illustrating Bible texts as well as typical Pennsylvania Dutch motifs, tulips, columns, dates, and identifications of the foundries that cast them. Some of the earliest stove plates were made at Thomas Rutter's Furnace, whose ironworks was set up in 1720, and they are among the earliest known and recorded in Pennsylvania. These rare and curious five-sided stoves were set half in and half out of the wall, and were known as jamb stoves. They were popular for their economical use of fuel, a plus that made them much in demand in that economy-minded area for half a century.

A similar type of decorative cast iron plate was set into the back wall of the fireplace and conducted the heat of the fire to the room behind the hearth, thus heating two rooms with one fire, a service

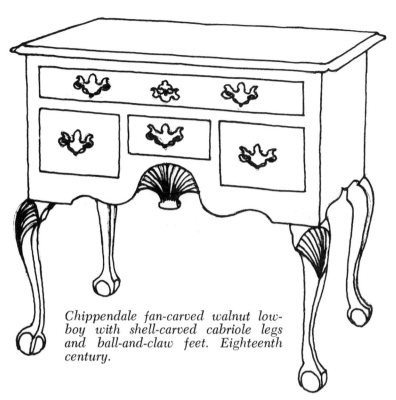

Chippendale fan-carved walnut lowboy with shell-carved cabriole legs and ball-and-claw feet. Eighteenth century.

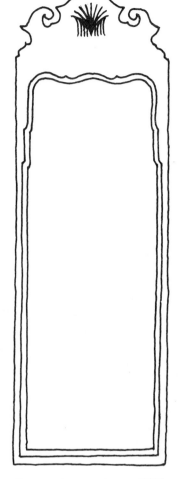

Queen Anne mirror. 1720.

the Dutch people highly approved of. Some of these wall plates were designed and cast by Stiegel, the well-known glassmaker, who at one time operated Elizabeth Furnace. Thomas Maybury, Hereford Furnace, Berks County, Pennsylvania, was another maker of these castings.

A short time later improvements and

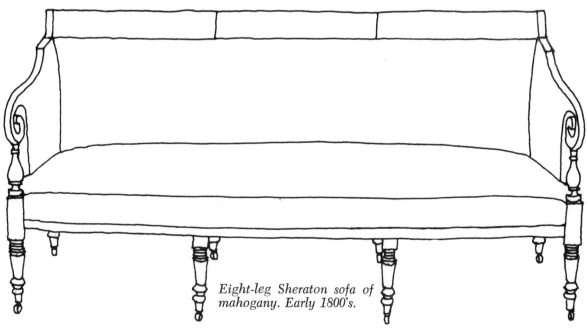

Eight-leg Sheraton sofa of mahogany. Early 1800's.

Brass andirons. The hexa-gonal standard is crested with a large urn finial and has spurred arched supports and ball feet.

Above. *Dunce-cap stove was patented in Pough-keepsie in 1816. Conical iron cap helped radiate heat. The fender, finials, and the collar under the cap are all of brass.*

Right. *Brass and wirework fireplace fender. 1700.*

changes were made on the primitive five-plate stove: the sixth side, a fuel door, and a stove pipe were added. Foundries now developed a stove that, except for the vent, was no longer attached to the wall. It was then quite a natural transition to Benjamin Franklin's ingenious stove—a movable half-stove, half-fireplace—cast by his friend Robert Grace at the Warwich Furnace. This ultimately became the fa-miliar Franklin stove, which is really an iron fireplace moved out of the wall of the house and into the room. As long as the stove pipe could reach the fireplace flue, it could be placed anywhere. From then on the changes in stoves and fireplaces ad-

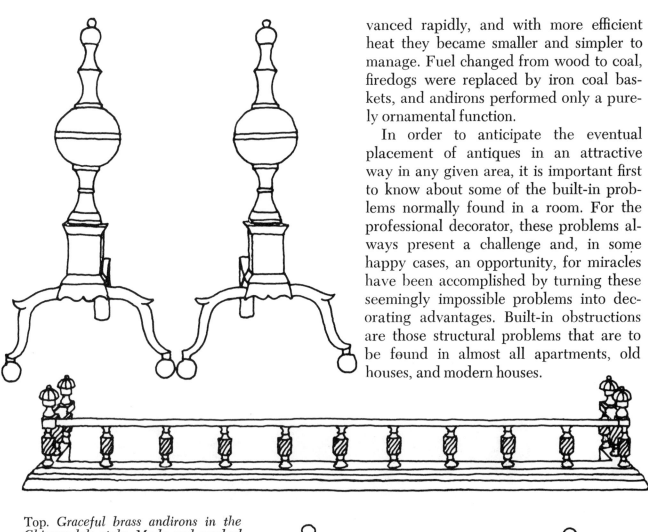

vanced rapidly, and with more efficient heat they became smaller and simpler to manage. Fuel changed from wood to coal, firedogs were replaced by iron coal baskets, and andirons performed only a purely ornamental function.

In order to anticipate the eventual placement of antiques in an attractive way in any given area, it is important first to know about some of the built-in problems normally found in a room. For the professional decorator, these problems always present a challenge and, in some happy cases, an opportunity, for miracles have been accomplished by turning these seemingly impossible problems into decorating advantages. Built-in obstructions are those structural problems that are to be found in almost all apartments, old houses, and modern houses.

Top. *Graceful brass andirons in the Chippendale style. Made and marked by Wittingham of New York. Marked brass andirons are rare in America.*

Center. *Brass fireplace fender, four feet long, with mushroom finials.*

Right. *Brass hexagonal melon-top andirons with bell-shaped finials. Boston. 1790.*

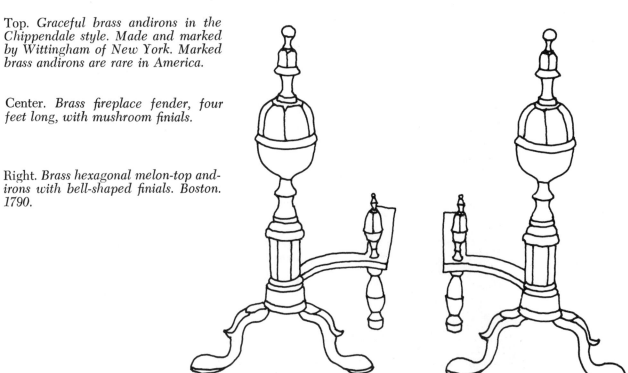

In authentic Early American homes, these problems are unique, but they are there. Doorways are small and low, as suited the more diminutive stature of the people of those past times. Doors invariably open the wrong way, and the windows, so symmetrically placed on the exterior of the house, have little reference to the need for light within. Windows were a luxury and the early builder used as few as possible in his construction. Somehow they always seem to be placed near a corner or on just the wrong wall.

The north walls of early Dutch houses were most often built to contain the chimney flue for the fireplace. This thick wall, devoid of windows, was planned as a protection for the people of the house against the winter wind. The New Englander, on the other hand, often placed his heating and cooking area in the direct center of the timber construction of his house so that the chimney could perform double duty as a flue for all the fireplaces in the center of the house as well as for the bake oven and, at the same time, support most of the inside beams of the house. Charming, yes, but this mammoth bit of heavy masonry took up as much as three hundred square feet of the floor space of these rather small houses.

This sort of structural built-in is not objectionable in itself. But in our expansive society, where a house is an indication of a need for room, this type of built-in has made expensive additional construction the general rule to add living space to the house.

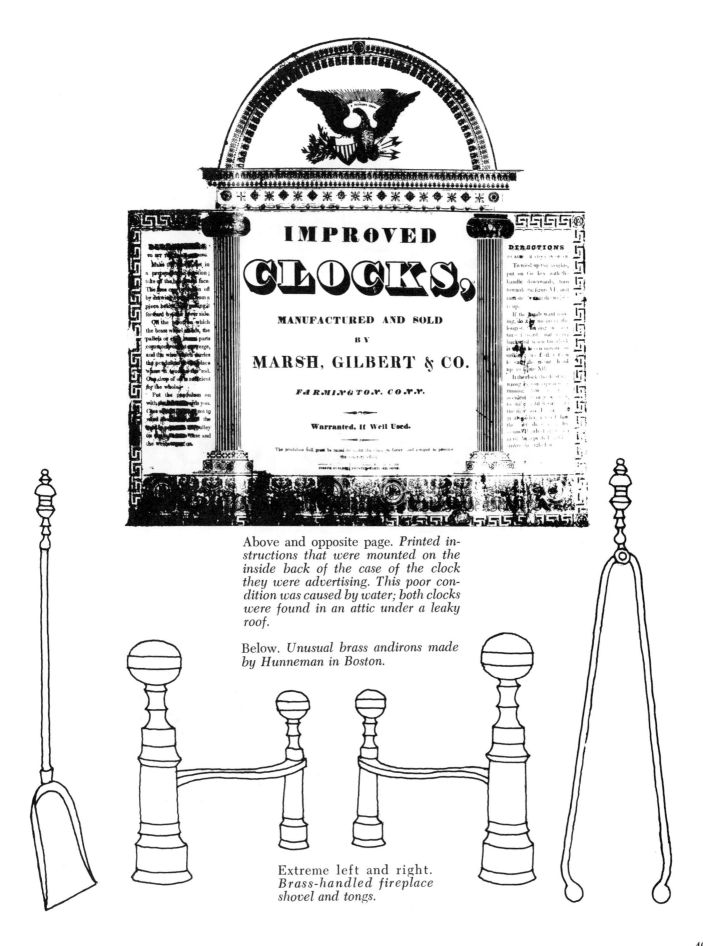

Above and opposite page. *Printed instructions that were mounted on the inside back of the case of the clock they were advertising. This poor condition was caused by water; both clocks were found in an attic under a leaky roof.*

Below. *Unusual brass andirons made by Hunneman in Boston.*

Extreme left and right. *Brass-handled fireplace shovel and tongs.*

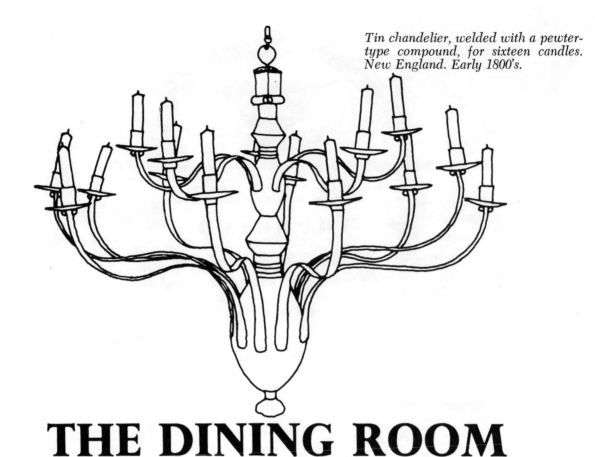

Tin chandelier, welded with a pewter-type compound, for sixteen candles. New England. Early 1800's.

THE DINING ROOM

Undoubtedly, it is the large expanse of beautifully polished wood in combination with sparkling glass and silver that makes a dining room so distinctively different in decor from the other rooms in a house. Although there are many other textures

Above. *Silver teapot with interesting ball feet. W. G. Forbes. 1805.*

Right. *Pear-shaped teapot, a fine example of New York silver. Adrian Bancker.*

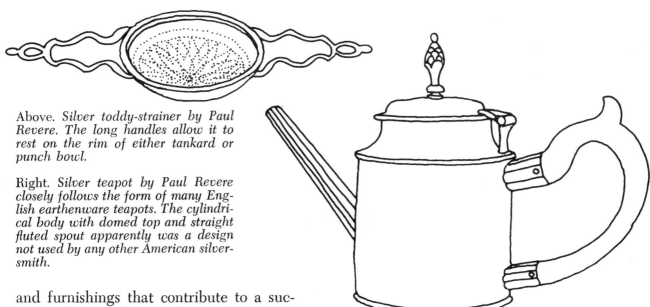

Above. *Silver toddy-strainer by Paul Revere. The long handles allow it to rest on the rim of either tankard or punch bowl.*

Right. *Silver teapot by Paul Revere closely follows the form of many English earthenware teapots. The cylindrical body with domed top and straight fluted spout apparently was a design not used by any other American silversmith.*

and furnishings that contribute to a successful dining room arrangement, the dining table itself presents such a dominant surface that everything in the room tends to direct itself to this handsome focal point—a highly sophisticated and acceptable decorating idea. People have been eating while seated at wood tables for thousands of years. It is little wonder that wood, and particularly polished wood, has such a satisfying emotional and visual effect on most people, particularly in the dining area. It is warm, it is basic and familiar, and on the practical side, china and silverware do not clatter on its surface.

Below. *Queen Anne mahogany drop-leaf dining table. 1730–1740.*

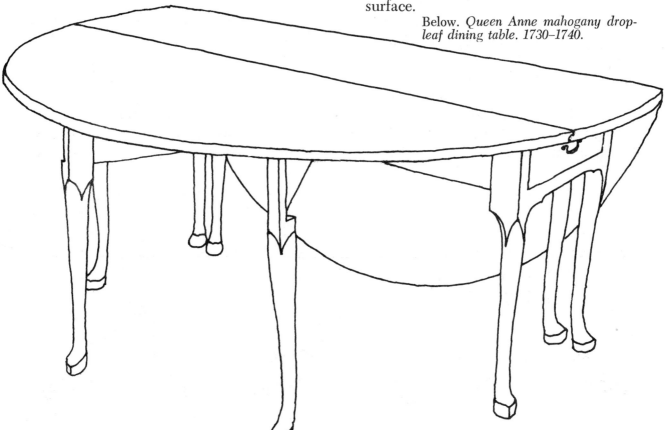

Above. *Silver candelabrum with shell pattern was one of the first made in Sheffield plate, 1812. With very slight variation this design continued to be popular for many years; specimens were turned out by the old process as late as 1850.*

Above. *Silver tankard by John Hancock, Charlestown, Massachusetts.*

Left. *Sheffield coffeepot. 1758.*

Wood was abundantly available in the early years of the Colonies; trees of huge size and of almost every variety were to be found. Their very diameter permitted planks of great width to be sawed from them. It was, in fact, ideal material for making the tables, benches, and other fundamental furnishings that the colonists needed for the daily ritual of sitting down to eat.

It is also little wonder that trestle tables, sawbuck tables, benches and other primitive furnishings, so much a part of the very beginning of our history, that were made at that time are so valued now. Nothing could be more American than

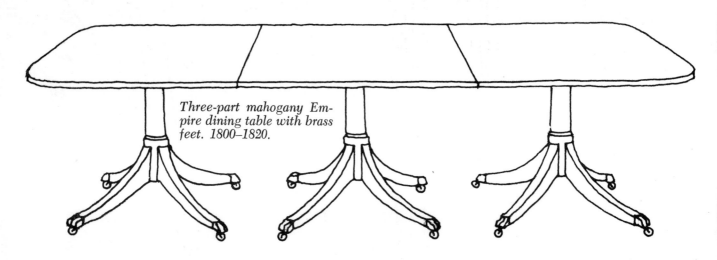

Three-part mahogany Empire dining table with brass feet. 1800–1820.

Above. *Rare Pennsylvania spice cabinet on wall is constructed with interchangeable drawers. Below it is a Berks County jelly cupboard. The dining table is also a bench.*

Below. *Berks County dower chest and decorated half-spindle chair. The compotes and celery are of baby thumbprint.* (Edwin F. Nimmo Collection, Barton, Pennsylvania)

Below. *This charming eating area is a converted smokehouse, part of a 1772 mill in Barto, Pennsylvania. The ice-cream-parlor set of chairs and table are hardly antiques—but just wait a while.*

Preceding spread. *The beautiful mahogany surface is an 1875 New Jersey banquet table with two drop leaves. It can be converted into two library tables. The pressed-glass candelabra are of the same period as is the hanging lamp with the painted shade. The cupboard is Pennsylvania Dutch from the middle nineteenth century. On the top shelf can be seen salt-glaze and Parian ware.*

Above left. *Decorated balloon-back chair and late nineteenth-century two-drawer butterfly cabinet. The mirror is Empire.*

Above right. *The willow ware is Buffalo and Staffordshire. The three amusing little figures are Staffordshire salts. The cabinet is early Pennsylvania Dutch, decorated with feather painting.*

Right. *The unusual child's highchair is painted and stenciled. Over it is a nineteenth-century barbershop kerosene lamp.*

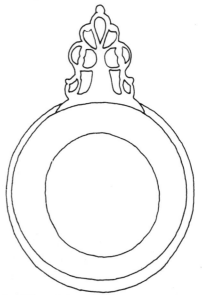

Left. *Little silver milk pot. On its side, Nathaniel Hurd of Boston engraved the owner's ship and mansion. Middle eighteenth century.*

Below. *Silver porringer by William Homes, Sr., nephew of Benjamin Franklin. Convex-sided bowl has a graceful cinquefoil-pattern "keyhole" handle. Boston. 1770.*

Far left. *Silver mug. 1740.*

Left. *Small, slightly bulbous, heavy silver mug with handsome scroll handle, molded rim, and folded flaring foot. Benjamin Burt, Boston. 1800.*

Bottom left, left to right. *Silver spoon handle of 1700 has a trifid (three-pointed) end; 1740 spoon developed a round-tipped handle, curved up at the end with a ridge down the center. The 1780 spoon handle turns down instead of up, bowl is narrower and more pointed, spoon thinner and lighter, handle sometimes decorated with engraving.*

these furnishings, designed and constructed by the earliest of the settlers of the Colonies and made from the very trees they had to cut to clear their new land.

The *Mayflower* could hardly be referred to as a furniture van, and for many years the small sailing vessels that reached the Colonies carried only the most important essentials. Furniture was not considered to be in that category. But fine oak and easier-to-work pine, the best raw materials, were so available to those earliest cabi-

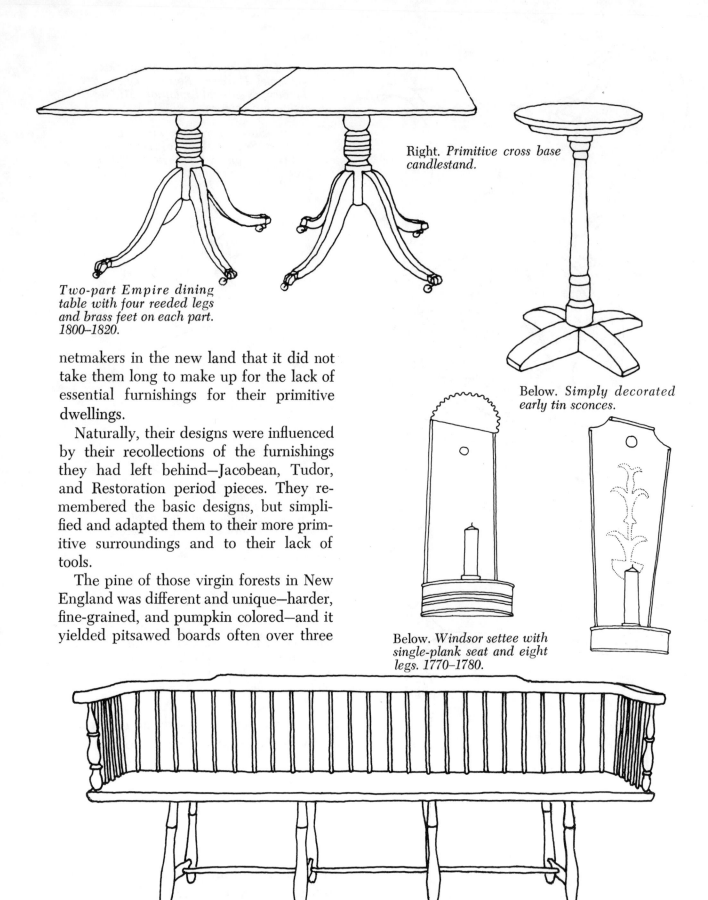

*Two-part Empire dining
table with four reeded legs
and brass feet on each part.
1800–1820.*

Right. *Primitive cross base
candlestand.*

Below. *Simply decorated
early tin sconces.*

Below. *Windsor settee with
single-plank seat and eight
legs. 1770–1780.*

netmakers in the new land that it did not
take them long to make up for the lack of
essential furnishings for their primitive
dwellings.

Naturally, their designs were influenced
by their recollections of the furnishings
they had left behind—Jacobean, Tudor,
and Restoration period pieces. They remembered the basic designs, but simpli-
fied and adapted them to their more primitive surroundings and to their lack of
tools.

The pine of those virgin forests in New
England was different and unique—harder,
fine-grained, and pumpkin colored—and it
yielded pitsawed boards often over three

Left. *Pennsylvania walnut corner cupboard with turned wood finials and brass "H" hinges. Eighteenth century.*

Windsor comb-back armchair with horseshoe back, excellent turnings, and a single center brace. Eighteenth century.

feet in width. The quality of this wood now simplifies the identification of some of the early primitive pieces, for today there are few trees and little wood of this same color and quality left in the whole of the United States.

Of course, fine furnishings were brought over from Europe at later dates and ultimately the colonial cabinetmakers in New York, Philadelphia, and Boston began to make important contributions to furni-

ture design. It was not long before the colonists had a successful and flourishing source of furniture from their more populated areas.

This country has been blessed with many fine silversmiths whose works rank with the best in that craft. Natural simplicity of design and little or no embellishment gave the silver articles produced by some of the patriots of Boston, Providence, Philadelphia, Baltimore—and, later, New York—a quality of lasting elegance.

Most American silverplate and other silver articles made by colonial silversmiths in New England and New Amsterdam are characterized by an unusual whiteness of the metal. This was probably due to the alloys used in West Indian sil-

Above. *Windsor child's high chair of the earliest type with a Queen Anne stretcher. 1720.*

ver coin, the silversmiths' basic source of the metal at that time. The coins were brought in by men who conducted a brisk trade between the West Indies and the colonial ports of New England. At about the same time, wealthy planters in the Southern Colonies, in true aristocratic fashion, had little desire to favor the northern craftsmen with their trade. They preferred to have their silver styled in England in the English tradition. The influence of English silversmiths on the co-

lonial craftsmen was thus inevitable. Indeed, they were willing to adapt themselves to it, for they wished to sell their products to the widest possible market.

One of the first collectors to recognize the important work of the colonial silversmiths was Judge Alphonso T. Clearwater, whose collection of items numbers in the hundreds and covers the period from the middle 1600's to the middle 1800's. The Clearwater collection and the important Garvan collection are perhaps the two most comprehensive American silver collections.

The Dutch, too, exercised an important influence on colonial silvermaking. They brought with them from Amsterdam an artistic heritage of hundreds of years. They were able to continue to produce their individual silver designs and styles by perpetuating the old-world apprenticeship custom, passing the craft from father to son.

Above. *Small corner cupboard with painted decoration.* (Metropolitan Museum)

Left. *An early Windsor chair with three-back waved-comb construction.*

Arch-back Windsor chair with one-piece bent back, braced with two extra spindles from tailpiece to crest.

As was stated above, it is not surprising that some of the English patterns were copied by the colonial silversmiths. Oddly, some of the copied pieces were put to an entirely different use than the one for which they had originally been designed in England. The American porringer is a typical example of an English design revamped for American purposes. Originally designed in England as a dish for medical purposes, its broad, single, triangular handle adapted well to the more prosaic and

Right. *Pennsylvania library-table with stretcher and scalloped apron. 1700–1730.*

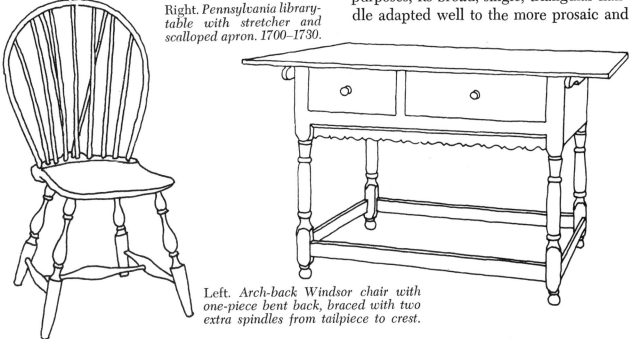

Left. *Arch-back Windsor chair with one-piece bent back, braced with two extra spindles from tailpiece to crest.*

Below. Fan-back Windsor with horned crest, two turned back uprights, and a turned "H" stretcher.

Above. Windsor chair with scrolled back, nine back spindles, handsome turnings. Pennsylvania.

Above. Braced arch-back Windsor, single bent piece for arms and back, turned "H" stretchers.

everyday needs of the colonist. The English style of intricately designed porringer handle soon gave way to simpler motifs. In the Colonies the handle was often designed around the owner's initials, and the bowl was set aside for his own private and express use.

It must be remembered that the Colonies had no assay office and only the maker's mark identified and guaranteed the quality and integrity of metal and design. While the New England settlers were using utensils of local materials and primitive manufacture, few wealthy planters in Maryland and Virginia were without a quantity of beautiful silverplate. Pewter was also used for dining and kitchenware, and most of the well-to-do Southern Colonial homes had a supply of both. Pewter alone was likely to be found in the less important homes. Unhappily, some of the finest early American silver pieces were lost forever when they were melted down

Maple and pine butterfly-table with single drawer, "whittled" pull. New England. 1710–1740.

and redesigned in the popular English styles, a practice not unusual at that time. Silver was essential to the life of the rich planter for it represented status and reminded him of his close ties to his Euro-

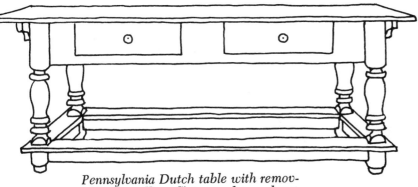

Pennsylvania Dutch table with removable "breadboard" top and two drawers. This type of stretcher table, often painted barn-red, is of a later date than the free-standing—leg table.

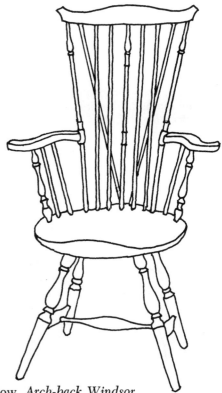

Below. Windsor chair with tenoned arms, delicate turning in middle of back and "H" brace was certainly not designed for comfort. 1760–1780.

pean background, a connection he did not want forgotten. Silver was decorative, utilitarian, and luxurious, in addition to being a secure investment in a country where the valuable metal was used for exchange.

The Windsor chair enjoyed a popularity in the United States that no other style has ever challenged. Often thought to be an original American design because it was made in this country as early as 1720, it had been made in England even before then. Because it was light, strong, and very comfortable, and because its construction was readily adaptable to the large range of available local woods, it was and still is acceptable in almost all settings except for the most formal.

Although there is now a tendency to refinish Early American furniture to expose the color and grain of its wood, the Windsor was originally painted, for it was made

Below. Arch-back Windsor with deep-cut seat has an interesting upward sweep to one-piece back and arms.

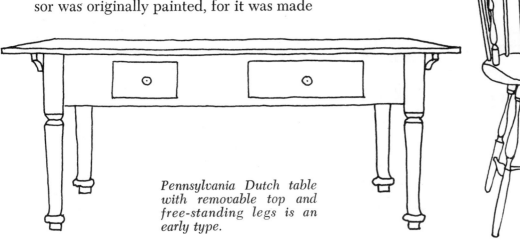

Pennsylvania Dutch table with removable top and free-standing legs is an early type.

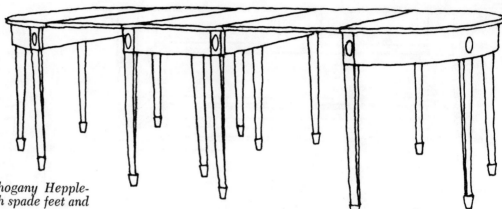

Right. Three-part mahogany Hepple-white dining table with spade feet and fourteen legs. 1790.

of several woods, each used for a special reason. The spindles were of ash, hickory or oak, whose long fibrous grains were easy to bend; stretchers were of maple or fine-grained wood that adapted to turning; and the ever-useful pine seat was simple for the maker to scoop out. The number of spindles added to the chair's comfort then and its value now; it is one of the details to look for in a Windsor.

Left. *Mahogany corner cupboard built to display fine china has tasteful carvings and "H" hinges. 1800.*

Above. *Six-paneled pine settle with scrolled apron. Pennsylvania or South Jersey. Eighteenth century.*

(A) *Molded slipware dish, initialed and dated 1794.* (Philadelphia Museum of Art)

(B) *Painted bird with glass eyes, carved of wood.* (Museum of Modern Art)

(C) *Decorative bird carved of wood and brightly painted. Pennsylvania.*

(D) *Gaudy Dutch Staffordshire china. Nineteenth century.*

The cant of the legs and a single brace connecting the two side braces holding the legs is an early construction detail; side braces connecting all four legs were a later feature.

Although most Windsors have now been refinished to the popular light finish, they were originally painted dark green and black, similar to the color of shutter paint of the same time. Construc-

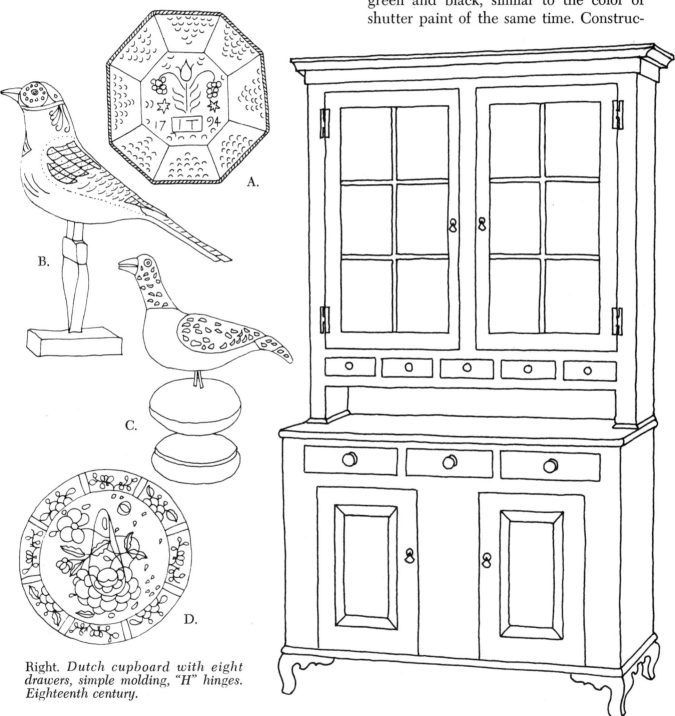

A.

B.

C.

D.

Right. *Dutch cupboard with eight drawers, simple molding, "H" hinges. Eighteenth century.*

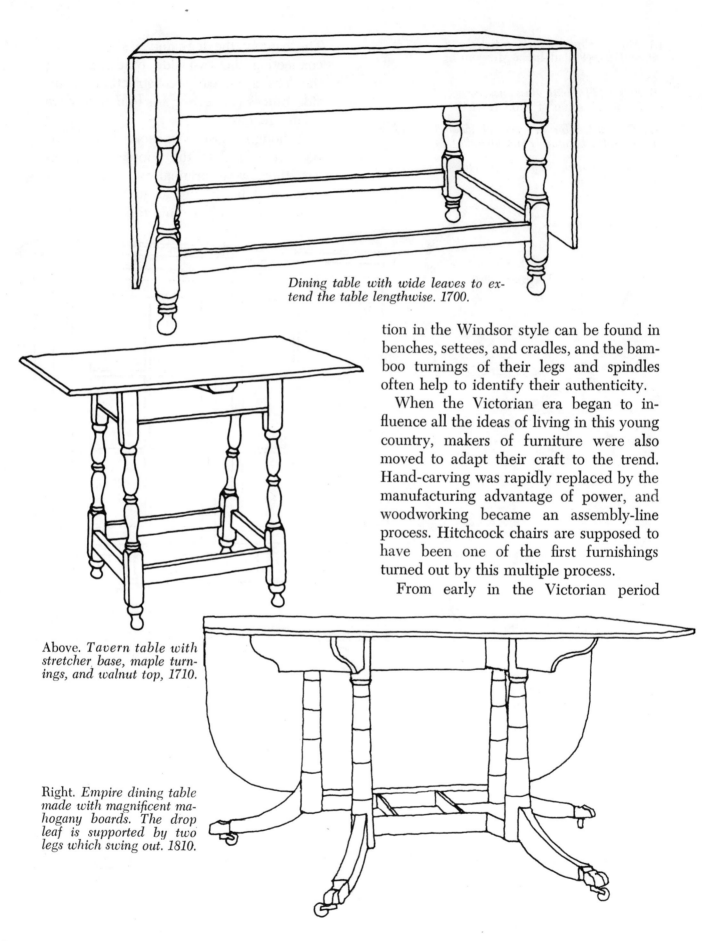

Dining table with wide leaves to extend the table lengthwise. 1700.

Above. *Tavern table with stretcher base, maple turnings, and walnut top, 1710.*

Right. *Empire dining table made with magnificent mahogany boards. The drop leaf is supported by two legs which swing out. 1810.*

tion in the Windsor style can be found in benches, settees, and cradles, and the bamboo turnings of their legs and spindles often help to identify their authenticity.

When the Victorian era began to influence all the ideas of living in this young country, makers of furniture were also moved to adapt their craft to the trend. Hand-carving was rapidly replaced by the manufacturing advantage of power, and woodworking became an assembly-line process. Hitchcock chairs are supposed to have been one of the first furnishings turned out by this multiple process.

From early in the Victorian period

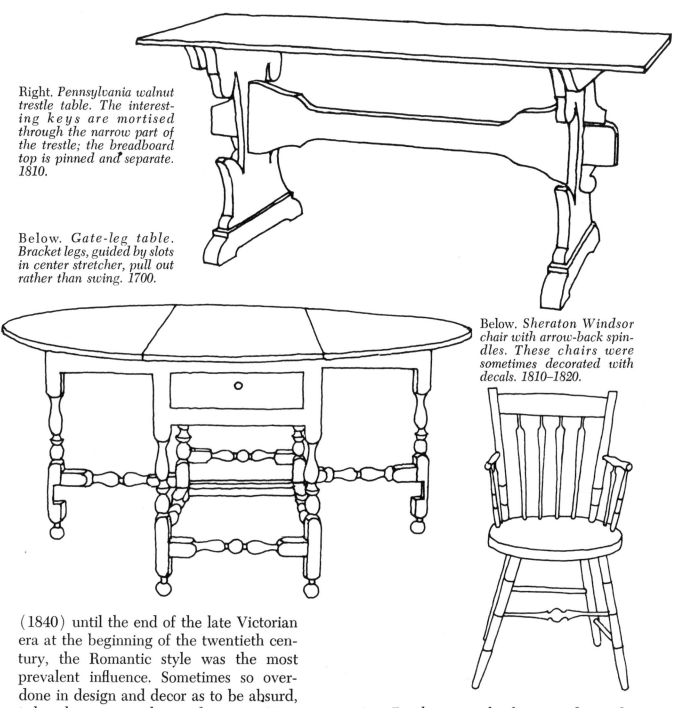

Right. *Pennsylvania walnut trestle table. The interesting keys are mortised through the narrow part of the trestle; the breadboard top is pinned and separate. 1810.*

Below. *Gate-leg table. Bracket legs, guided by slots in center stretcher, pull out rather than swing. 1700.*

Below. *Sheraton Windsor chair with arrow-back spindles. These chairs were sometimes decorated with decals. 1810–1820.*

(1840) until the end of the late Victorian era at the beginning of the twentieth century, the Romantic style was the most prevalent influence. Sometimes so overdone in design and decor as to be absurd, it has, however, a charm of its own. Now that primitive antiques are less available to the casual collector, this Victorian period of Americana is the main source of many of the antiques yet to be found.

Following the Revolutionary War, the popular Federal style came into its own. The eagle—painted, carved, or inlaid in marquetry—was the most popular decora-

tion. By that time the fruit woods, apple and cherry, as well as maple and satinwood, were in use, and a small quantity of Central American mahogany was being brought in by the enterprising clipper ship trade for the cabinetmakers' use. About 1810, Duncan Phyfe, probably the most popular and certainly one of the best known and most prolific American

A-B. Typical Stiegel-type salts, made commercially.

C-D. Midwestern salts, which were made in large quantities by bottle houses.

E-F. Nineteenth-century commercial salts, also made in large quantities; they preceded pressed-glass salts.

Right. Glazed pottery figures of cock and hen. Pennsylvania. Eighteenth century.

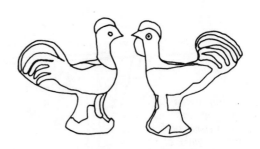

A.

B.

C.

D.

E.

F.

Above. *Pennsylvania dresser with scrolled cornice and end boards rat-tail hinges on paneled doors. The upper shelf is a spoon rack. Eighteenth century.*

Left. *Painted chalk deer. Bucks County, Pennsylvania. Early nineteenth century.*

cabinetmakers, began turning out works bearing his name. Deeply influenced by Sheraton, the English Regency style and, in some places, the French Directoire period, Phyfe was reputed to have employed as many as one hundred workmen in his factories. Quantitatively alone, he would naturally have had a great influence on the design of furnishings of that period.

Above. *Eagle-pattern ironstone tureen with separate welled platter is marked "Imperial White Granite Gelson Bros. Hanley, England."*

Below. *Eagle-pattern ironstone cocoa pot. This same design was carefully adapted to all the pieces of this unique ironstone ware set.*

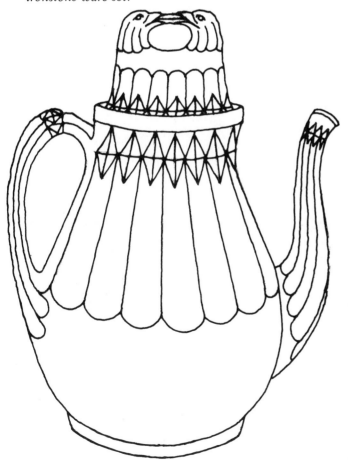

The colonials, who bought the works of the finer cabinetmakers, were the pace setters of style and fashionable living then, just as there are pace setters now. Obviously, the people interested and financially able to indulge themselves in collecting in those times were of more than average wealth. The country was largely populated by people who had left generations of the better things of life behind them to build a new life in America and those financially or politically able to maintain a position of power and luxury in the New World were few. More often than not, they also brought with them some of the less attractive European ruling class attitudes.

Their opinions were inclined to be positive and certainly they were not to be argued with. We must remember that the majority of people in this young country were much more concerned with survival than with ideas about artistic expression. When a man of prominence judged an article of furnishing or bric-a-brac to be good or bad, he was simply expressing his own personal taste. It is a happy accident of those times that the talent of the artisans made the judging easier; more of the

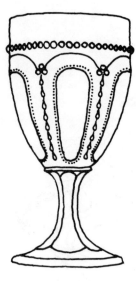

Left. *Beaded dewdrop pressed-glass goblet. 1840 to 1900.*

objects made then were better designed and constructed than during any subsequent periods of our history.

Time, of course, is an important factor, for the fact that an object was a part of our history is sufficient to make it important. But time does not necessarily make man-made things better; it simply causes them to be judged by a different set of standards. If however they have the best qualities of design, function, construction, and historical background they will be valued indeed.

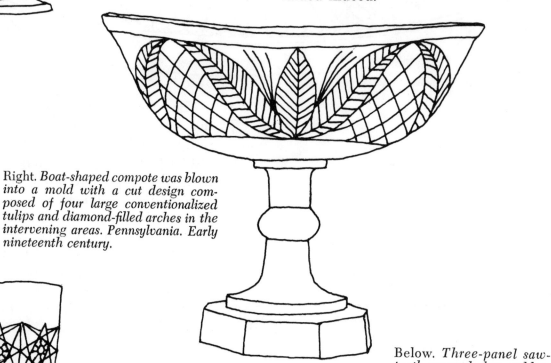

Right. *Boat-shaped compote was blown into a mold with a cut design composed of four large conventionalized tulips and diamond-filled arches in the intervening areas. Pennsylvania. Early nineteenth century.*

Above. *Octagonal goblet with daisy-and-button design.*

Below. *Three-panel saw-tooth pressed-glass goblet.*

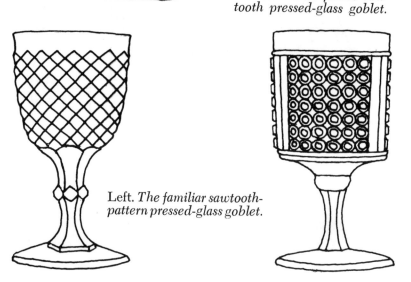

Left. *The familiar sawtooth-pattern pressed-glass goblet.*

New England bull's-eye pressed-glass goblet.

Above. *New England pineapple pressed-glass goblet. 1840–1890.*

Above. *Tulip-pattern pressed-glass goblet.*

Right. *Bull's-eye with fleur-de-lis pressed-glass goblet.*

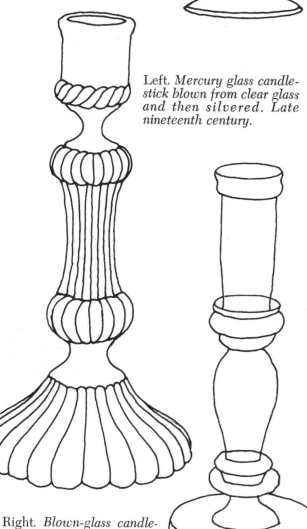

Left. *Mercury glass candlestick blown from clear glass and then silvered. Late nineteenth century.*

Right. *Blown-glass candlestick. New York. 1831–1850.*

It is only recently that primitive artistic expression has become so acceptable. Technique and craftsmanship are often thought of simply as adjuncts, welcome but not absolutely necessary.

Today people surround themselves with things that they enjoy living with, and so, regardless of expert opinions, the choice of what antiques you want to own and collect is yours alone. A hundred years from now, your choices may just have made an expert out of you.

One early self-styled expert made the same mistake that anyone will make if he does not take into consideration the test of time. Furthermore, he compounded the error by putting it in writing. In an article on the subject of pressed glass, he said that Sandwich glass, which enjoys great favor in America today, was popular with the poor folk or plain people and was a type of glass to be found mainly in the cabins of the lower classes. As a writer and collector of antiques in the nineteenth century, he really should have thought of the importance of change.

We must take into consideration that this statement was made over seventy

Below. *Mocha mug. Black and sepia or blue and green on cream or café au lait are the traditional colors for Mocha ware, a soft-paste porcelain made in England and imported to America.*

Above. *Footed Mocha-ware pitcher in brown and blue "seaweed" pattern.*

Above. *Mocha pitcher with "seaweed" decoration.*

years ago. Needless to say, it is certainly not accurate by today's standards of judging glass. We might add that the arrogant tone and negative references to people would not be tolerated today. The statement itself is, however, an interesting picture of some of the people who were leaders then and, as historic reference, it is valuable despite its somewhat egotistical overtones and obvious lack of foresight.

There has always been a constant re-evaluation of what is collectable and what is not. There were few if any well-to-do collectors in our early history who would have given house room to a spinning wheel or a butter churn. These objects were utilitarian and, as such, were not considered in the same light as they now are by anyone fortunate enough to own one.

Right. *Mocha-ware pitcher with cover may have been used for a cocoa pot.*

Below. *Rockingham-type yellow-ware pitcher, New Jersey. Mid-nineteenth century.*

Below. *Mocha-ware pitcher decorated with bandings of cat's-eyes and "serpentine" ropes.*

Right. *Mocha bowl.*

We would certainly never deny the great importance of classic pieces and all their essential characteristics: beauty of concept and design, fine craftsmanship, materials of excellent quality, and the signature of the famous maker still intact.

But everything made cannot come up to these standards. Indeed, it was not essential for a dough tray made for a Pennsylvania housewife to have any of them, save sturdy construction; but as a matter of history that dough tray must be given its proper due.

With this country's population now over the two hundred million mark and the economic level high, a great many Ameri-

Left. *Sgraffito plate with bird or "distelfink" design.*

Right. *Sgraffito plate with popular eagle pattern. 1830.*

Below, center. *Primitive slipware plate, simple in design, the colors limited to white, black, and green on a red-brown background. Pennsylvania.*

Bottom right. *Sgraffito plate with the tulip design so popular in Pennsylvania.*

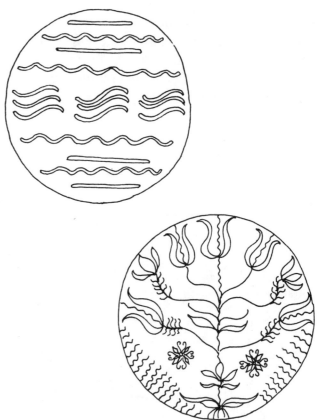

Left. *Early open-shelved pine kitchen dresser of simple design with scroll work. Single door "H" hinges are of forged iron.*

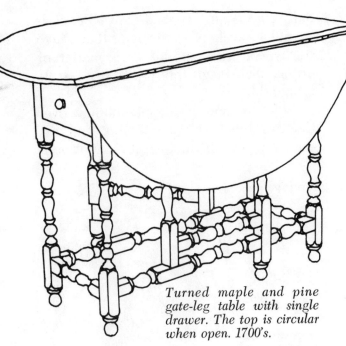

Turned maple and pine gate-leg table with single drawer. The top is circular when open. 1700's.

When we quote them, it is only to show that even then people thought this subject was important. They believed that their opinions were right and that their advice was good. The following quote was written by a highly respected nineteenth-century antique collector. He warns us against indiscriminate purchases and is scornful of the direction that his countrymen's sudden interest in antiques at the turn of the century was taking: "the outpourings from farm houses of fancy egg dishes in the shape of sitting hens or dilapidated and worthless old pewter and other atrocities of cheap American factories of the nineteenth century." The items cans now have a chance to own something of our country's past.

To read the warnings of the early collectors and writers on the subject is to recognize that learning about antiques is important, but the decision as to what to collect and what will become more valuable as time goes on must be made by each buyer alone.

Our research continually brings us into contact with articles and books on antiques written in the nineteenth century.

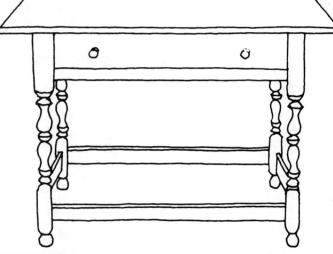

Above. Maple and pine tavern table. Full-length drawer has two peg pulls. 1700.

Left. Splay-leg walnut dropleaf table. Western Massachusetts. 1700.

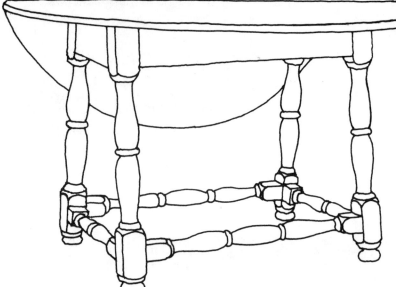

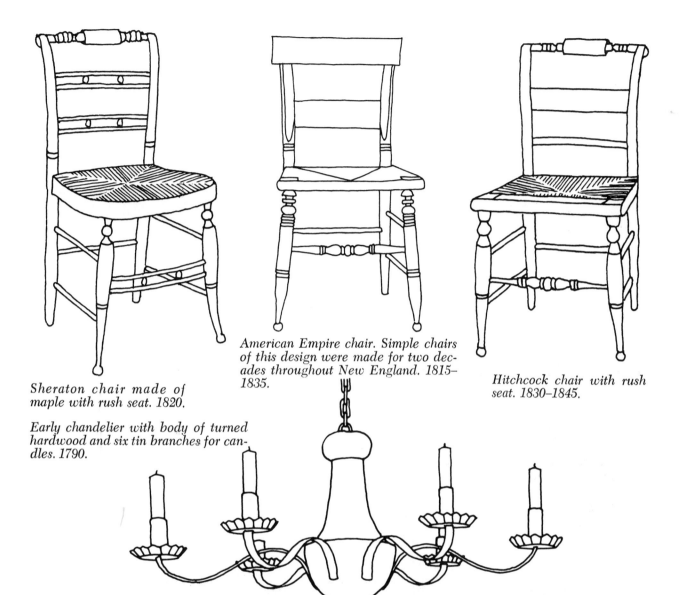

Sheraton chair made of maple with rush seat. 1820.

American Empire chair. Simple chairs of this design were made for two decades throughout New England. 1815–1835.

Hitchcock chair with rush seat. 1830–1845.

Early chandelier with body of turned hardwood and six tin branches for candles. 1790.

mentioned negatively in the quote are now considered to be collector's items, and properly so. This causes one to pause and look around him to discover which of the contemporary objects he now owns will, if preserved, become meaningful items of curiosity or beauty and value to the generations to come.

When we study the beautiful furnishings from the better homes of colonial Philadelphia and New York and from many of the elegant homes of the south, we find two famous makers well represented: Duncan Phyfe, of New York, and William Savery, of Philadelphia, both master craftsmen much influenced by the English manner and material of cabinetmaking.

We must also remember that a great variety of gilded and carved furnishings in the Chippendale style were made by imitators who produced rather large quantities of furniture in factories located in most of the major urban areas. As the style and fashion in furniture shifted to Sheraton and Hepplewhite; it became as difficult for even the experts to separate the work of the original cabinetmakers from their imitators as it was to distinguish work produced by American craftsmen from pieces made by London cabinetmakers.

Left. *Pewter pitcher, seven and one-half inches high, was made somewhat in the style of the old tankards.*

Above. *Queen Anne–style pewter teapot, made in Philadelphia. Late eighteenth century.*

Right. *Pewter teapot. Early nineteenth century.*

Left. *Serpentine open-top corner cupboard in the Queen Anne style. Single paneled door is fitted with rare, forged iron butterfly hinges.*

When early antiques writers touched on the subject of furniture again the future had no part in their writings. They scorned the cabinetmakers in rural places who made plain furniture out of cheap materials such as pine, maple, and walnut for the country folk—furnishings that were surely destined for poorer homes and farmhouses. The error in their writings is not so much that they did not foresee the future, for that would be asking a lot, but that they, as self-styled experts, did not see the simple beauty of the sturdy utilitarian furnishings made from local wood. These very same pieces are pre-

Far left. *Primitive pewter oil lamp, probably used as a bedroom light.*

Left. *Pewter flagon. The handle, lid, and thumb pieces are of English design while the body shows Teutonic influence. Lancaster County, Pennsylvania. Late eighteenth century.*

Right. *Pine corner cupboard with fluted base pillars and split column turnings on top portion. Pennsylvania.*

ferred by some collectors over any of the other styles and makers of our short past.

The fact that these humble pieces made of local woods by nameless cabinetmakers have at last become so desirable and valuable proves once again that the history of an object often transcends its other qualities, and that its acceptance over a long period of time can be a true indication of its worth.

In all fairness, of course, it would have been impossible for the early critics to have foreseen the complex suburban and exurban life style of the twentieth century and to have known of the vast market for these very same pine, maple, and walnut pieces, so beautifully adaptable to our present kind of country living.

On the subject of glass, and especially fine glass, most experts agree that there are some pieces that have all the qualities

(A) *Porcelain vase made in New York in 1816 is probably the earliest true porcelain made in the United States.*

(B) *One of the many Toby jug characters.*

(C) *Slipware vase or "bulb kettle" was used for sprouting onions out of its openings. (Philadelphia Museum of Art)*

(D) *Salt-glaze earthenware money bank. Late nineteenth century.*

(G) *Sgraffito drinking mug with the popular tulip motif. Pennsylvania. 1816.*

(E) *Salt-glaze earthenware pitcher. 1891.*

(F) *Earthenware pitcher, made in Cincinnati, Ohio, marks the beginning of contemporary "artware." 1883.*

of art. Wistarberg, which was brought forth in classic flint glass in Salem County, New Jersey, in approximately 1739 (at least twenty-five years before the Stiegel glass factory was built) is one such.

Henrich Wilhelm Stiegel, another master glass craftsman and innovator, came from Cologne and settled in Philadelphia in 1750. Stiegel purchased his father-in-law's iron furnace in Lancaster County and with the profits opened his glass works in Mannheim, Pennsylvania, in 1764. After the passage of the Stamp Act of 1765, the products of the American Flint Glass Manufactory were greatly sought after by the New York and Philadelphia markets They were particularly valued for their

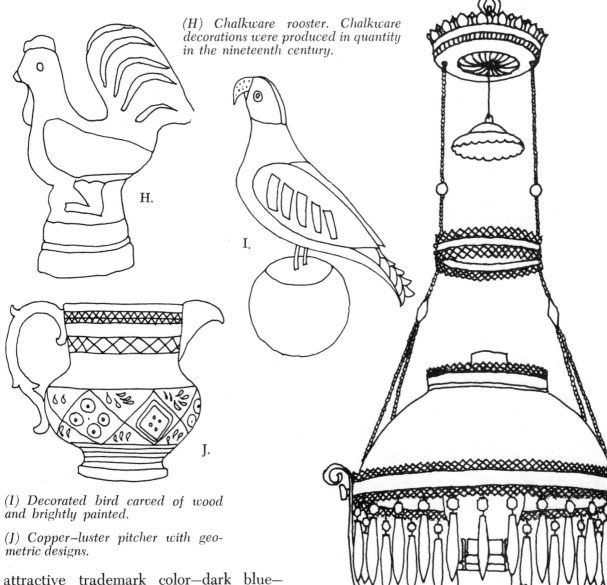

(H) Chalkware rooster. Chalkware decorations were produced in quantity in the nineteenth century.

H.

I.

J.

(I) Decorated bird carved of wood and brightly painted.

(J) Copper–luster pitcher with geometric designs.

attractive trademark color—dark blue—which was as identifying a characteristic as the green glass of Wistarberg.

Glassmaking, so much a part of our colonial history, is a subject as broad as furniture making. Later, we will talk about some of its early beginnings in more detail, because it is important to know a bit about the background of each of the categories of American antiques. In your search for pieces that are still available and of good quality, a knowledge of historic background will be of great help to you in your final decision to purchase or not to purchase.

Glass has had one of the most humble beginnings and longest histories of all ob-

Victorian hanging lamp with plain shade, brass frame, and brass kerosene fount. Girandoles are of pressed glass, the smoke bell is brass. The lamp can be raised or lowered by a spring counterbalance in the topmost piece.

New England stenciled tin tray.

jects. Made of fused sand and common soda, it is said to have been used as the hardening of glaze on pottery as early as 5500 B.C. Thus its history is almost as ancient as civilization itself. Objects of glass were exported from Alexandria and Tyre during the time of the Roman Empire. The blowpipe and the tonglike tool the glassblower uses for shaping glass were discovered around the first century B.C. and have remained relatively unchanged for almost two thousand years.

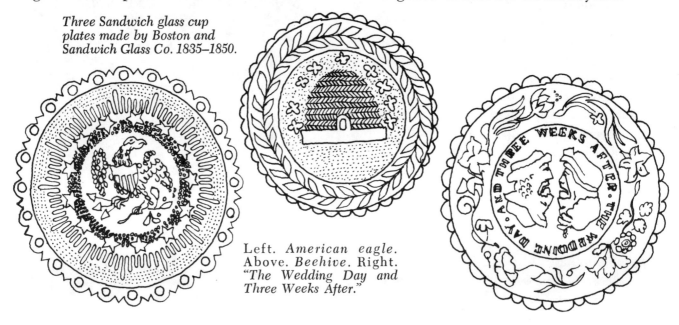

Three Sandwich glass cup plates made by Boston and Sandwich Glass Co. 1835–1850.

Left. *American eagle.* Above. *Beehive.* Right. *"The Wedding Day and Three Weeks After."*

Left. *Early side-wheel steamship.* Below. *American eagle and stars.* Right. *Oak leaf and acorn wreath.*

Three Sandwich glass cup plates made by Boston and Sandwich Glass Co. 1835–1850.

Below. *Painted tin tray depicting steam locomotives. Pennsylvania.*

The history of glassmaking covers the entire geography of Europe and much of the East, where it was said to have begun. Venice, Germany, France, the Low Countries—and, later, England—practiced this art. Each country changed the forms to satisfy the local nobility who popularized glass and brought it to the attention of wealthy and interested people in their countries. Colorless glass of lead or "flint," which gave glass a new brilliance and caused it to be less brittle, thus making it easier to cut or engrave, was developed in England. In 1674 Charles II granted recognition to George Ravenscroft and gave him a patent for the manufacture of a crys-

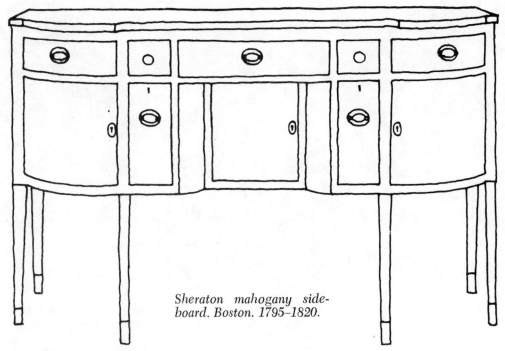

Sheraton mahogany sideboard. Boston. 1795–1820.

talline glass with a rock-crystal quality, and the right to manufacture articles of this glass for English consumption and for export. Thus, several decades later, many of the new American colonists had been exposed to English glassmaking and were already familiar with the qualities of this superior glass. When colonial glassmakers began to blow their own fine table and ornamental glass, a great proportion of it was lead glass made from this same English formula. Because most artisans of glassmaking came to the Colonies from Europe, they brought with them the tech-

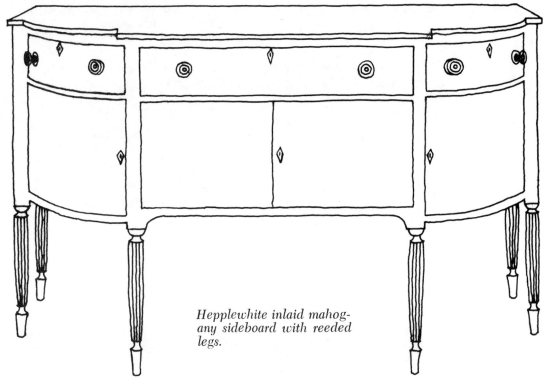

Hepplewhite inlaid mahogany sideboard with reeded legs.

Right. *Primitive tin lamp with four branches for candles. Berks County, Pennsylvania.*

Above. *Gilded pier glass* Constitution *mirror with picture of the frigate in the lower bay of New York Harbor.*

Right. *Carved and gilded half-spindle Empire mirror.*

niques and ornamentations characteristic of their places of origin. Although two styles of glassmaking—the English and the German—predominated in the Colonies, it was not long before a distinctive American flavor became apparent in the glass houses of Pennsylvania, New Jersey, and New Amsterdam. It is also a historic fact that a primitive type of American glass was blown during the time of the Virginia Colony of Jamestown, long before George Ravenscroft was born. History records

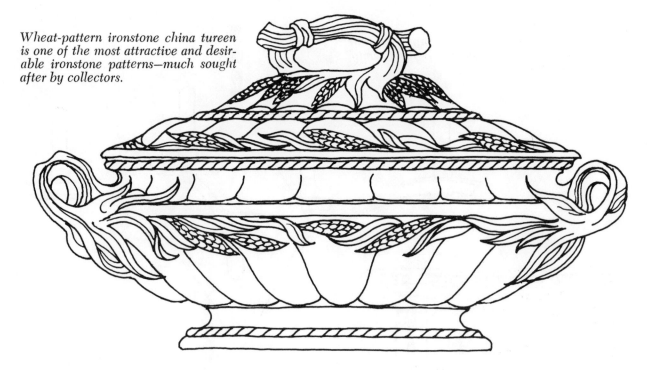

Wheat-pattern ironstone china tureen is one of the most attractive and desirable ironstone patterns—much sought after by collectors.

that there was an ambitious plan in this same early colony to make goblets and articles of glass for export to England, a plan that was, fortunately, never carried out.

In glassmaking, wood is necessary for making of potash soda and for the head needed to fuse the sand. The Colonies, with unlimited quantities of sand and timber, appeared to be the ideal location for the manufacture of this highly exportable product. There is much recorded of the glassmaking venture in Virginia, and it is

a fascinating sidelight into the history of that colony.

By the early eighteenth century, there were eight or ten glass houses of note in the Colonies, but only several of them seem to have survived the troubles of that time and registered as important producers. The glass houses of Caspar Wistar and Henrich Wilhelm Stiegel were two of the most important. There are, of course, books solely devoted to the history and the output of these two great colonial glassmaking pioneers; both the historic

Below. Simple ironstone tureen. These were made in great quantity in Victorian times and were not always part of a set but were individually designed.

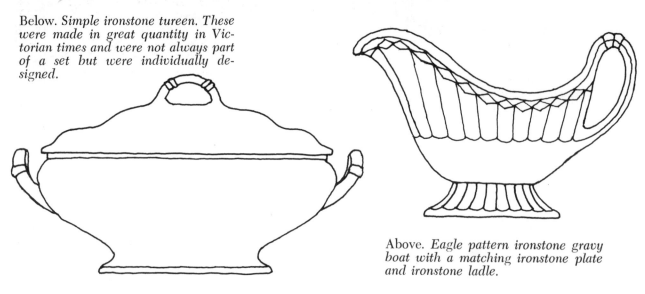

Above. *Eagle pattern ironstone gravy boat with a matching ironstone plate and ironstone ladle.*

Above. *Ironstone gravy boat with welled plate. Late Victorian. Below. Ironstone tureen; one of many patterns made in quantity.*

Below. *Large round ironstone tureen, gracefully scrolled. Its cover is topped with an apple-shaped knob and leaves. Late Victorian.*

and the romantic details of this art and of its founders' lives make fascinating reading.

Stiegel's flint-glass house, completed in 1769, specialized in tableware and at its

peak employed over one hundred men, many of them master blowers, flowerers or engravers, cutters, and enamelers. Widely marketed and advertised throughout the Colonies, it was favored by patriots resisting the English Stamp Act of 1765 for its products were by and for the colonials. Purchase of objects of English manufacture was considered unpatriotic.

Below. *Three-part mahogany Sheraton table with reeded legs. Center part holds two deep drop-leaves. 1820–1840.*

THE KITCHEN

Ordinarily, a chapter on the kitchen would be the natural place to start a book about living with antiques, for the kitchen is where living in houses really started. Indeed, it is where living together started, even before there were houses. People came together around the fire for warmth, food, companionship, and dreams. It is not strange that many of the early artisans directed their talents toward articles used in the preparation and serving of food. Ease of use, gracious dining and en-

tertaining aids, and utensils of beauty all followed later. Many of today's important dining-room luxuries can be traced to the humble early kitchen.

The following illustrations of these articles show some antiques that are still not hard to find. Prices vary: Some of them are still a steal, whereas others are very costly. But there is one thing that you may be sure of: Because they are American antiques, you will derive pleasure from living with them, and time will make

Above. *Pennsylvania Dutch table with removable top, stretcher base, and two deep drawers was originally covered with red paint.*

Opposite page. *Large Willow platter.*

Above. *Brass-based table lamp with opaque shade was very popular and was manufactured and distributed widely.*

Above. *Late Victorian bracket lamp with pressed-glass kerosene fount and shade. This design was made up until the late nineteenth century.*

them increasingly valuable, so that eventually none of them will have been an extravagance.

The kitchen is often a room of buzzing activity—it functions at full speed at least three times a day. It must have all those items that the period in which one lives can offer to make the work of preparing food as easy and as efficient as possible. This was as true two hundred years ago as it will be two hundred years from now. An abundance of useful and practical appliances does not necessarily mean that a kitchen has to be thought of as, and look like, a machine shop.

In the first place, it is the fundamental family room. It is where all those good things you eat come from. It is where mother can usually be found. It should look as attractive as the food a good cook serves. We know that the way food is presented is essential to its appetite appeal, and the same is true of kitchen appeal.

For good reason, antiques were made with much the same idea in mind. When a cooking utensil was made, it was wrought strong and practical, with design factors that made it individual. Sometimes the design was as simple as an extra small curl in the forging of a spoon handle or a blue-glaze bird on the side of a stoneware pickle crock. Uniqueness of design is the major charm of many of the hundreds of cast-iron trivets and hand-cut butter molds. Cookie cutters made in shapes to please the children increase the pleasure of eating the cookies. Glass jars with tight-fitting ground-glass stoppers for storing flour, sugar, or staples of any kind have not, as practical containers for everyday use, been bettered by even the most modern packaging. Today's package designs

Above right. *Stoneware crock with cobalt-blue slip decoration on typical gray salt-glaze color. Mid-nineteenth century.*

are for store shelf display and storage, and are hardly made to be decorative pieces on permanent display in the kitchen.

Because the kitchen is filled with appliances necessary to modern living, it becomes a challenge to make it attractive.

Left. *Stoneware jar with cobalt-blue bird was used for cider, vinegar. 1820.*

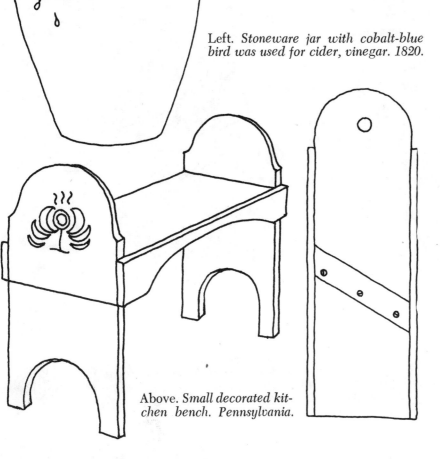

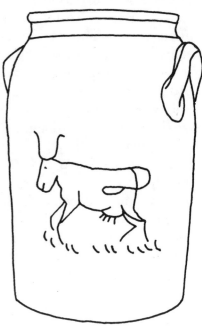

Above. *Salt-glazed earthenware jar with cobalt-blue cow motif.* (Landis Valley Museum)

Left. *Pennsylvania Dutch cabbage cutter.*

Above. *Small decorated kitchen bench. Pennsylvania.*

Above. A kitchen shelf is a good place for these early blown jars, for they can be seen and appreciated while performing a utilitarian duty. The Seth Thomas school clock is as practical as the late Victorian clock on the left is impractical. The Leeds platters and the heavy tin mold are on display when not in use.

Right. Small shutters cover shelves and the Bennington jugs add a touch of color. The top pitcher is quite unusual—New England, 1840.

Below. Noodle board and kitchen utensils are Pennsylvania Dutch and the forgings are particularly fine and unusual. The noodle board is of chestnut and is as practical for today's baking as it is decorative.

Above. *The trestle table and benches are primitive. The wood trough from Massachusetts is maple and very early. The copper bucket is a type used in the making of apple butter since the eighteenth century. The half stove-plate seen standing in the fireplace is early Penn-* *sylvania Dutch, as is the redware on the fireplace mantel. The dry sink on the extreme right is early Victorian and was still being used for its original purpose when purchased in 1958.*

Left. *Scrapple pans certainly haven't changed in two hundred years, and the same is true of the pudding steamers. The spice shelves on the far left are not original but seem to be an adaptation of an early cutlery shelf.*

Bottom right. *The cabinet is the top of a very early piece. The rattail hinges and handmade moldings are primitive. Ironstone and tin molds of the nineteenth century can be seen. The lamp is late Victorian brass and pressed glass.*

Right. The hinged doors that covered a fireplace are, indeed, a fortunate find. The delicate iron match holder casting is from New England. On the mantel is a late Victorian coffee grinder. The sickles are on the kitchen wall purely for their fine forging and not for kitchen use. The noodle board is walnut and typically Pennsylvania Dutch.

Below. The second view of this kitchen is to show the late Victorian stove (Roman Apollo), still practical to use, but preferred for its decorative qualities. These turn-of-the-century stoves are rapidly becoming extinct.

Left. *The Dutch cabbage cutter behind the Victorian bracket lamp is walnut and quite primitive. The wheat pattern in the pudding mold is deep and clear. They all look particulary good together when the spice boxes are added for color.*

Below. *Willow ware is both attractive and practical. The kitten-ear arrow-back chairs and cherry drop-leaf table in foreground are of the middle nineteenth century. Buffalo willow ware is American and very desirable. Early willow can be found in a type of pottery that is much like paste ware in texture. Staffordshire was only one of the English makes and it is deep in color and sometimes resembles flow-blue.*

Too often the kitchen takes on the sterile quality of an operating room and lends little to the living and togetherness that are so much a part of this most-lived-in room.

When we move things about in the kitchen, as we do periodically in all the rooms of the house, it is not simply because we are restless or because of our lack of decision in decorating. We are just changing things around to reanimate our surroundings and give the whole a new look. All we really try to do is to place those objects we have collected where we feel they will please us most and show to their best advantage.

If any one of these objects becomes too

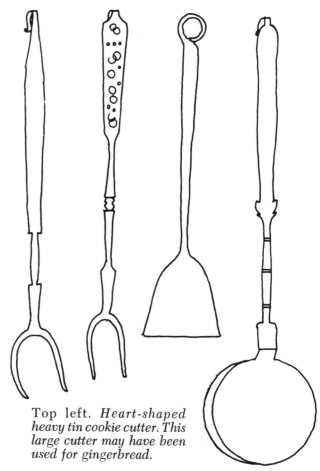

Top left. *Heart-shaped heavy tin cookie cutter. This large cutter may have been used for gingerbread.*

Above. *Wrought-iron culinary utensils: forks, flapjack shovel, and ladle. Pennsylvania.*

Large walnut gate-leg table of extremely sturdy construction has two gates on each side.

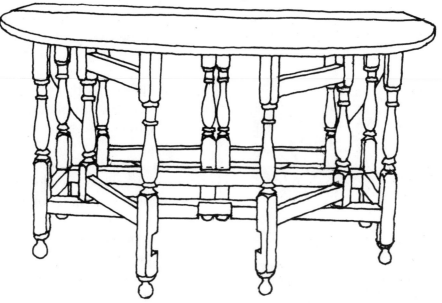

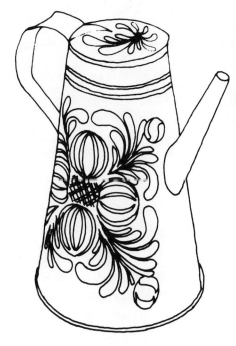

Above left. *Decorated tin apple tray with rolled edge. New England.*

Above right. *Painted tin coffeepot. Lebanon, Pennsylvania.*

Left. *Painted and decorated tin milk pitcher. Lebanon, Pennsylvania.*

Below left. *Painted cookie box with "distelfink" motif. The hasp is typical of Pennsylvania Dutch tinware.*

important in the room, we have failed. It is our desire to collect things we like and place them where they can be enjoyed and will make the room a totally unified and attractive place to live and work in. If there is to be a dominant note in most rooms, please let it be the people who live there. In the kitchen the dominant idea is the preparation of food, and everything in it should direct itself to that end.

As more than interested antiquers, we are not exclusively dedicated to any particular period or subject relating to antique collecting. That kind of accumulating proves nothing but tenacity. It is also most expensive to attempt to corner the market on any single category of objects in the antique world.

Right. *Decorated wooden box. Ephrata, Pennsylvania. 1800.*

Below: *Decorated coffeepot of heavy tin with small brass knob on lid. Typical early Pennsylvania Dutch motifs.*

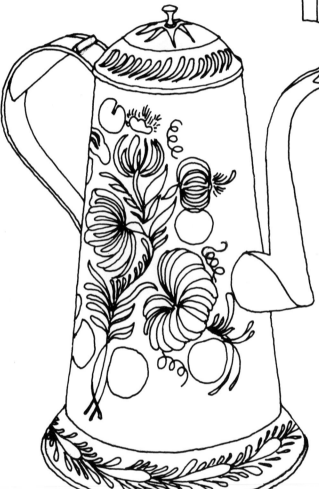

We also feel that it is wasteful to surround oneself with things that are temporary. As average Americans with a family, we, too, are caught up in today's world of appliances and disposables, and often we like it and know they are essential to comfortable living. But for the furnishings, utilitarian or purely decorative, that you choose to spend your life with, you should enjoy as much long-lasting comfort and beauty as you can afford. If we have limited ourselves in the choice of the objects *we* prefer, it is Colonial Americana.

We don't particularly care whether the articles are primitive, classic, early or late Victorian, just as long as they are basically American. We believe in mixing and matching these periods and styles to suit our taste with only slight regard for their original uses. We are not afraid to combine them with articles of a more modern America when we feel it is right. The at-

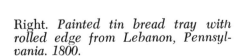

Right. *Painted tin bread tray with rolled edge from Lebanon, Pennsylvania. 1800.*

Ornamental flatiron stands. Decorative iron castings can be found in many patterns and were cast until the end of the nineteenth century. Early twentieth century patterns advertised their makers and were made in cast iron as well as sheet iron.

tractiveness of the whole room is the desired result and each individual piece will make its proper contribution if placed imaginatively. Decorating a room is a way of expressing oneself and not simply the job of displaying a collection of articles of fine craftmanship. Placing antiques under glass, lighting them with spotlights, allowing them to be observed at a respectful distance is precisely the job for a museum.

But we suggest that you collect only the antiques you really want to live with. What difference if their backgrounds are English, German, French, Dutch, or whatever, or if some of the ideas were developed a bit earlier than others, for what they are is an important part of what

makes all Americans what we are. It is only important to like the antiques you acquire and to put them together in a tasteful way in your home. The kitchen, where we spend so much of our time, is certainly no exception to this rule.

Surely the craftsmen of early times felt the same way. Particularly in Pennsylvania, much of the earliest ware was made specifically for the housewife's needs and comfort. The craftmanship was characteristic of the worker's background, but he borrowed ideas from the more progressive seaboard communities. These workmen turned out fine and useful articles with their own inimitable decorative signatures.

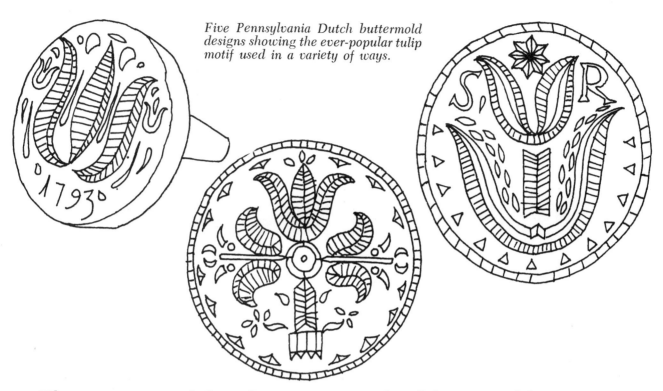

Five Pennsylvania Dutch buttermold designs showing the ever-popular tulip motif used in a variety of ways.

When we see some of the techniques used to decorate pewter adapted to the ornamentation of tinware by the Pennsylvania tinsmiths, we see this borrowing in action. Tinplate was not made in the Colonies until after the Revolutionary War. Much of the "Gaudy Dutch" attributed to colonial tinsmiths was of English make, as was the Staffordshire china of the same period. The color and the crude technique of the Pennsylvania Dutch tinsmiths can in no way compare with the fine finish of English toleware. The English had long been manufacturing and exporting great quantities of this popular ware and had

perfected the process of decorating it to a high degree.

Tin sconces, designed both to hold the candle and to reflect its light, were a part of the tinman's wares, but these rather simple and decorative pieces were copied right up until modern times, as were cookie cutters of the same material. It would take a metallurgist to ascertain if they were made in colonial times or not.

Beverage pots were designed by the Dutch tinsmiths for coffee rather than tea; their forms were probably adapted from earthenware coffeepots of the old country rather than from English tole-

Above. *Pennsylvania Dutch pie safe. The ventilated cupboard with wood frame and top was covered with panels of perforated tin and used for storing pies and other baked goods.*

Right. *Two punched-tin coffeepots have traditional motifs combined with Victorian touches.*

ware teapots of the eighteenth century. But they were charming and colorful in spite of crude workmanship. Their brightly painted surfaces were covered with the favorite symbols of Pennsylvania—tulips, birds, and flowering branches, punched out in tiny raised dots in a technique used to decorate pewter. Because a great many of these utilitarian pieces were made to order, the date and name of the recipient were added in the same style and technique as the all-over design. Sometimes a small brass knob or finial added a charming finishing touch of bright metal that resembled gold. The "pie safe," or cupboard, another article unique to the

Pennsylvania Dutch, can still be found in dealers' shops. Their wood-frame forms are covered with tin or zinc, with geometric designs punched through the metal to permit ventilation of the interior shelves on which were stored baked goods and other foods. This kept the food in fresh air and yet safe from mold, flies, insects, and four-legged predators.

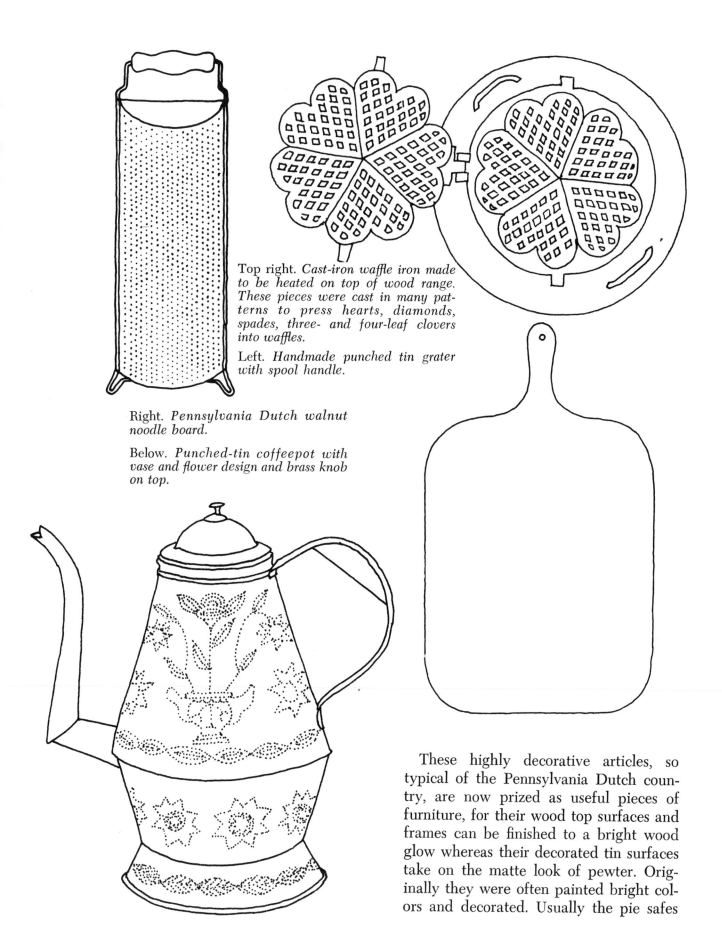

Top right. *Cast-iron waffle iron made to be heated on top of wood range. These pieces were cast in many patterns to press hearts, diamonds, spades, three- and four-leaf clovers into waffles.*

Left. *Handmade punched tin grater with spool handle.*

Right. *Pennsylvania Dutch walnut noodle board.*

Below. *Punched-tin coffeepot with vase and flower design and brass knob on top.*

These highly decorative articles, so typical of the Pennsylvania Dutch country, are now prized as useful pieces of furniture, for their wood top surfaces and frames can be finished to a bright wood glow whereas their decorated tin surfaces take on the matte look of pewter. Originally they were often painted bright colors and decorated. Usually the pie safes

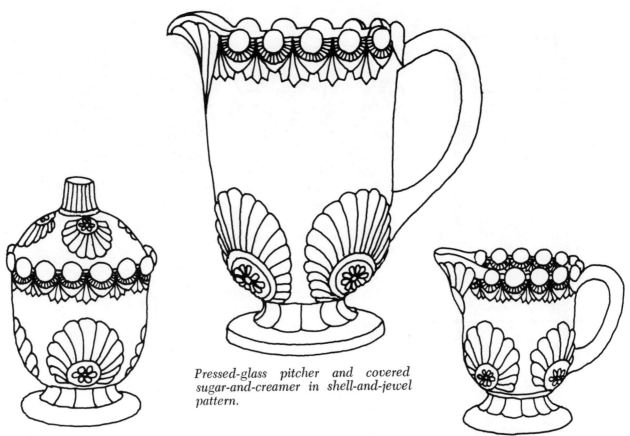

Pressed-glass pitcher and covered sugar-and-creamer in shell-and-jewel pattern.

were made with one or two doors that opened to the shelves, making storage space readily available. With the attractive and practical punched tin sides, no one need worry about mustiness. The punched tin area of these cupboards cov- ers all four sides leaving only the top, usually of table height, a flat wood surface. In some cases, the four supporting corner posts protrude above the top. The cupboard was constructed this way so that it could be hung from cellar beams, keeping the food stored inside cool and safe and off the damp cellar floor.

Splay-legged table with scrolled ogee skirt. Leaves are supported by slides. New England. 1700.

Pennsylvania kitchen table with maple legs and removable pine top. The "H" stretcher shows early construction. 1710–1750.

Until the latter part of the eighteenth century, a good majority of finished-metal plate articles were of English manufacture. The Colonies were permitted to smelt ore, but prohibited by English law from roll-

ing it into plate. However, the local foundries had quantities of raw or pig metal, with which they cast or forged stoves and kettles, cranes, and all forms of utensils for the country people. The bright and light importations from England were left for the housewives in the towns. It was not unexpected, however, that the country folk soon discovered these colorful and highly practical articles, although they might only have been exposed to them on the annual trip to town to replenish stores of items they could not make themselves. These colorful articles of fine English tinware proved to be irresistible even to the thrifty Pennsylvania housewife.

Shell-and-jewel–pattern pressed-glass tumbler, spoon holder, covered butter dish, and pedestal cake plate.

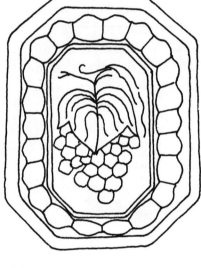

Left. *Painted tin syrup container with bottom set in to hold heavy weight of syrup. Cap fits over flange Pennsylvania.*

Above. *Heavy molded tin pudding steamer. This cooking utensil has changed very little in the last two hundred years. It is still produced in copper and tin.*

Right. *Deep ceramic pudding mold in grape pattern. Molds were made in a variety of patterns in the mid-nineteenth century.*

Below. *Coffeepot and heater of painted tin. Nineteenth century.* (Philadelphia Museum of Art)

Ironware was most important to the cooking or fireplace area. The crane, a gate-like object of forged metal, was hinged into metal eyes that were set deep into the brickwork at the back of the fireplace. The crane was able to swing out of the fire area and over the cool hearth. Thus, the pots suspended from it were not directly over the flame, making it easier for the housewife to remove them comfortably.

The trammels, with their sawtooth adjustments, and the cooking chains that hung from the crane enabled the cook to adjust the distance between the cooking pot and the flame. This had the same effect on cooking that turning the flame itself up or down has now. All these vital "appliances" were forged by smithies of great skill, who added individual designs, shapes, and delicate forgings of decorative quality. It would be impossible to find

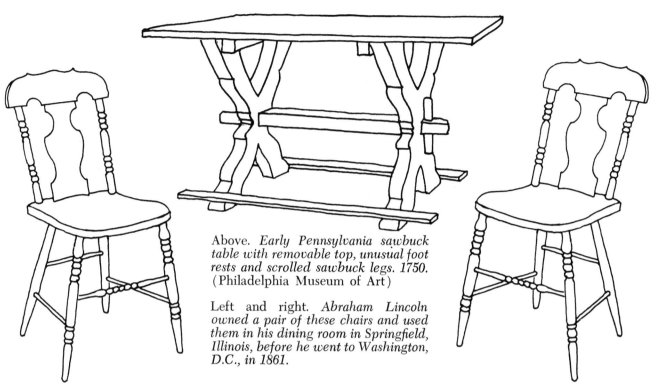

Above. *Early Pennsylvania sawbuck table with removable top, unusual foot rests and scrolled sawbuck legs. 1750.* (Philadelphia Museum of Art)

Left and right. *Abraham Lincoln owned a pair of these chairs and used them in his dining room in Springfield, Illinois, before he went to Washington, D.C., in 1861.*

two trammels or cooking chains identical in forging, design, or ultimate function, for they were made to correspond with the height from the hearth of each individual crane in the main fireplace of each primitive dwelling.

The cooking vessels themselves were totally utilitarian. Spiders, or iron frying pans, were well designed and almost inde-structible. Three long forged legs added to the base of the pan gave the user the option of more or less heat by the simple method of raising or sinking the legs into the hot ash bed of the fire.

It was common practice at that time for people to harvest or buy their staples in bulk much the same as a farmer does to-day. Because of the quantities of produce,

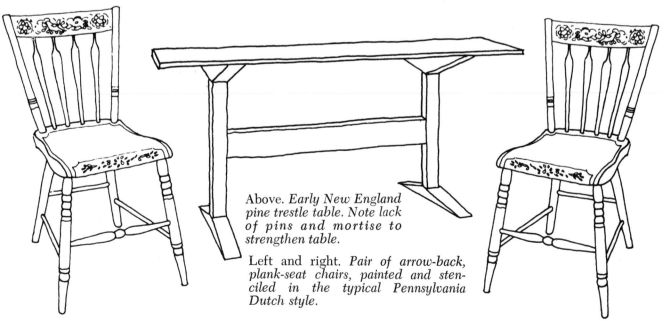

Above. *Early New England pine trestle table. Note lack of pins and mortise to strengthen table.*

Left and right. *Pair of arrow-back, plank-seat chairs, painted and stenciled in the typical Pennsylvania Dutch style.*

it was necessary to have adequate storage containers. The same is relatively true today, for even in the smallest kitchen of the smallest family there are staples needed for everyday use that must be kept in bulk. These staples might well be stored and displayed in blown- and pressed-glass containers that are both practical and attractive—containers that can become an important part of the decorative and functional needs of the kitchen.

If any room of the house lends itself to simple antiques made of wood, it is the kitchen. The warmth of wood is right in

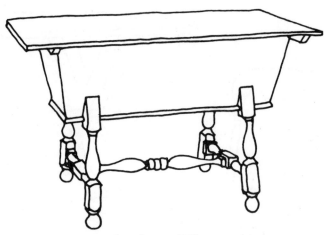

Above. *Pine dough tray. When mounted on legs as this one is, it was called a "dough trough." Pennsylvania. Eighteenth century.*

Left. *Early eighteenth-century New England pine corner cupboard with paneled front and sides, double door in base, and wrought-iron "H" hinges.*

kitchens. An old wall school clock or late Victorian mantel clock may not add anything to the flavor of the jiffy muffins you just dropped into the pop-up toaster, but it might just keep alive the good old feeling one had in times when mother's or even grandmother's slow-baked, whole-grain bread warmed and cheered the whole house.

The kitchen does need adequate light for preparing food and manipulating knives and appliances. Unfortunately, although both proper lighting and modern appliances are well designed for kitchen use, they are not always aesthetically appealing. But when the cooking is over and the utensils for preparing and serving the meal are put away, there is no reason why the kitchen cannot be as attractive as any other room in the house.

There are many objects of Americana that are only now capturing the collector's attention. Here, imagination plays an important part in your collecting. To recognize value in objects that have been passed by for years because they did not carry

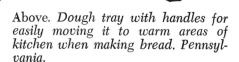

Above. *Dough tray with handles for easily moving it to warm areas of kitchen when making bread. Pennsylvania.*

the maker's name or the benediction of an expert is a skill that will make collecting an even greater joy for you.

What difference if that attractive coffee table on your porch was at one time a wooden stretcher used by the Dutch people for processing hams? Now well-polished and with heavy plate glass covering

its top, it will serve its new purpose admirably and last at least another hundred years. What does it matter if this former hog carrier is surrounded by comfortable wood rockers of arrow-back construction or shovel-back country chairs with plank seats? Why not hang a simple kerosene lamp above the table for light? Certainly the lamp found will not be of Stiegel glass, but it is early American and bound to be charming and fun for the people who sit around it. What's so wrong with adding a rocking chair made of decorative wicker from the late Victorian period to the scene? Unconventional decorating? Per-

Below, top. *Rock maple rolling pin. Early New England.* Below, center. *Salt-glaze Pennsylvania Dutch rolling pin. Handles can be removed and cylinder filled with cold water when rolling out dough.*

Above. *Deep, heavy tin cake mold, in the popular rope design of the Pennsylvania Dutch.*

Left. *Primitive pine rolling pin. Central Massachusetts. 1760.*

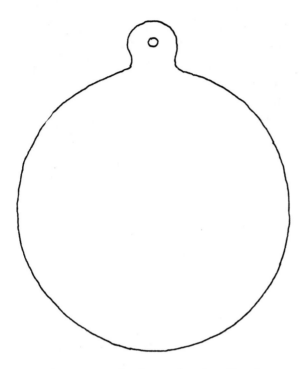

Two typical Pennsylvania Dutch noodle boards. Upper one is heavy one-inch pine, and lower is made from a single piece of walnut. Both are approximately eighteen inches across.

haps. Imaginative? Certainly. Fun? Absolutely!

It makes little difference to your guests if the glass pieces on your mantel are priceless antiques that might be found in a museum's glass collection or if they are pressed glass from the late 1800's, as long as they give the mantel area an interesting effect. Certainly, later pieces can be replaced with earlier and finer ones as opportunity and funds make this possible and/or desirable. But somehow or another one can become just as attached to a pitcher and glass set of carnival ware as one might be to a similar set of priceless Tiffany. They are antiques you found yourself and bought because you liked—a very satisfying set of circumstances. Should you at a later date find and be able to afford Tiffany to replace your lesser treasure, you will certainly be able to sell your old set, perhaps at a profit, to either the original seller or a new purchaser, for Americana is always increasing in value.

Right. *Pennsylvania Dutch cabbage cutter with removable blade was used for shredding cabbage for sauerkraut.*

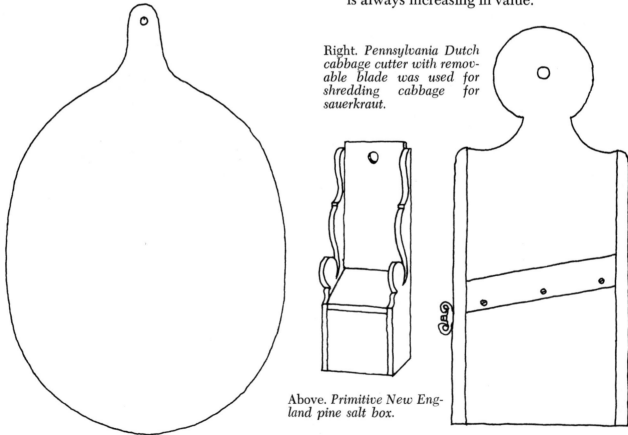

Above. *Primitive New England pine salt box.*

Ironstone dishes and platters do not have to be of wheat pattern or classic duckbill for everyday use. A myriad of lesser-known patterns of later periods of manufacture are available and are made for daily use. They are almost always marked or stamped on the back. These were not called "ironstone" casually. It is not surprising that these sturdy and simply designed pieces of china have withstood time and usage. Again, they are not as valuable or fragile as early paste ware or Pennsylvania Dutch redware, but they do belong to early and late Victorian times and their stark whiteness and simple design do much to enhance a table. They have the clean look and feel that goes so well with quantities of good, wholesome, homemade food. Antique

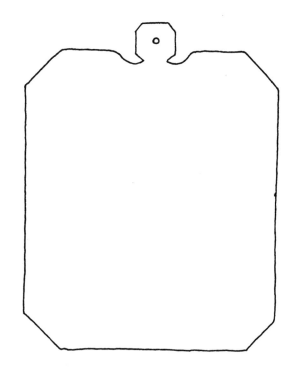

Two Pennsylvania noodle boards. Upper one is of chestnut and lower of walnut. Later boards were made of heavy slate, mined and made in Berks County. Pennsylvania.

Two Pennsylvania Dutch cabbage cutters, made of walnut. They are of sturdy construction and were used constantly.

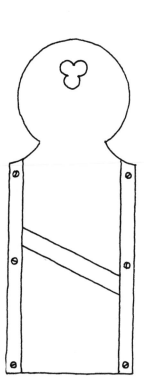

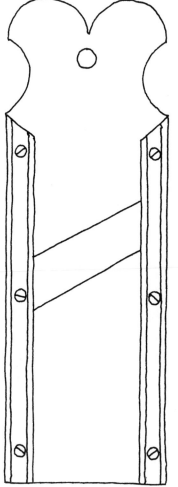

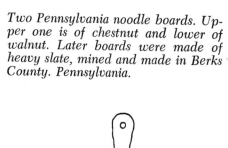

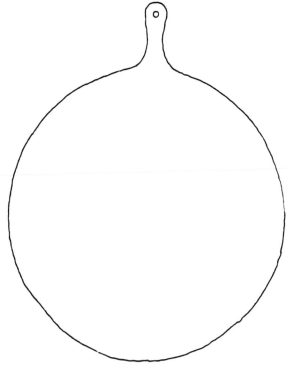

breadbaskets with a clean white napkin folded inside are just right for holding hot biscuits or rolls. It makes no difference if the rolls come from the supermarket freezer, for the very look of these sturdy little baskets will make what they display taste all the better. It is interesting to note that these little straw baskets originally held bread made of rye flour, for the farmer almost always sold his wheat for cash. Thus, his staff of life was the less expensive bread, made of coarse rye grain and served in baskets constructed from the straw of the same plant.

Though saltshakers as we know them

Right. *Pennsylvania Dutch cutlery rack.*

Below. *Wrought-iron kitchen utensils: skimmer, ladles, forks, spoons, and flapjack shovels.* Top row left *shows front and back of flapjack shovel.*

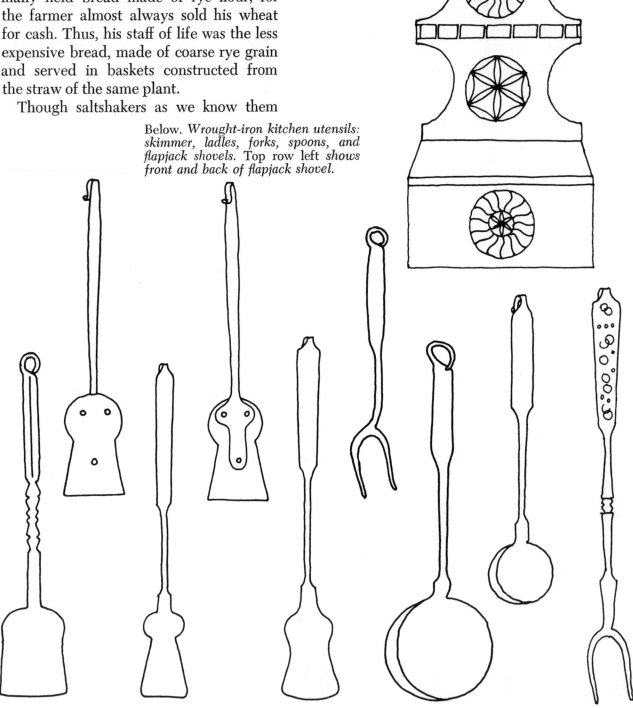

date back to a very early period, the salt box was for the colonists the sole guardian of that precious commodity. Hanging prominently on the wall of the kitchen in a warm and dry place, it was a sign of well-being, for salt was expensive and hard to come by. It was, for a long time, the only seasoning the settlers had for their food. It is no wonder that it was looked upon as a sign of affluence and its container was decorated with carvings and polychromed with the best of the Pennsylvania decorations and colorful symbols.

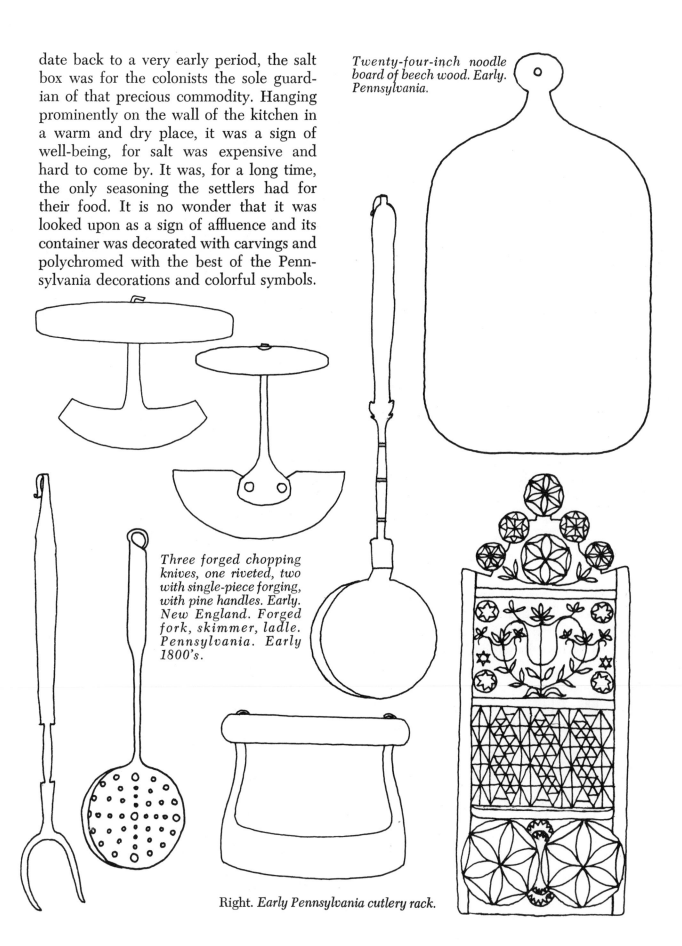

Twenty-four-inch noodle board of beech wood. Early. Pennsylvania.

Three forged chopping knives, one riveted, two with single-piece forging, with pine handles. Early. New England. Forged fork, skimmer, ladle. Pennsylvania. Early 1800's.

Right. *Early Pennsylvania cutlery rack.*

Tin cookie cutters made in both New England and Pennsylvania are practical for present use. They are much sought after by collectors.

In early Victorian times when salt was presented to the head of the table, it was contained in fine glass dishes called "master salts." The salts were about the size of a small dessert dish and can still be found in a variety of pressed-glass designs. Later, when this table service was expanded to individual salters so that each guest

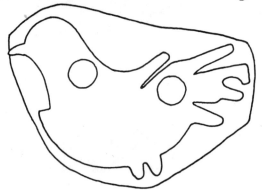

might serve himself as many pinches of the seasoning as he wished, the glass market took another giant leap. Sandwich and many other glassmakers made salters of pressed glass, now highly prized collector's items. Master salts were made by many of the fine glassmakers, and can be seen in some of the important collections.

The manufacture of salt sets continued for a great many years. During late Victorian times tiny silver salt spoons were introduced from England to eliminate the use of fingers from the ritual. This kept the salter in use many years longer. If anyone is fortunate enough to have a set of salters and their little silver spoons, they would still be a charming touch to add to the dining table.

Now that we have free-running salt, the shaker is again with us. If one were to attempt to catalog the shapes, sizes, and types of pressings, blown glass, and overlay glass, not to mention silver and pewter, that have been formed into saltshakers, it would be a life's work. Almost every manufacturer has made items to take care of this everyday need.

Cabbage cutters, most essential in the Dutch country, were made to grate cabbage into slaw, which was then fermented in wood casks. The slaw was pressed down by a heavy flat stone that covered the entire top of the cask. The cutters, made mainly of wood and single or multiple forged knives, were in sizes varying from small kitchen utensils to giant cutters that fitted over the casks. They had sliding boxes that held three or four cabbages to be grated at one time. The wood frame was decorated with as many different colorful motifs as there were items made for kitchen use. Sturdily constructed, the cab-

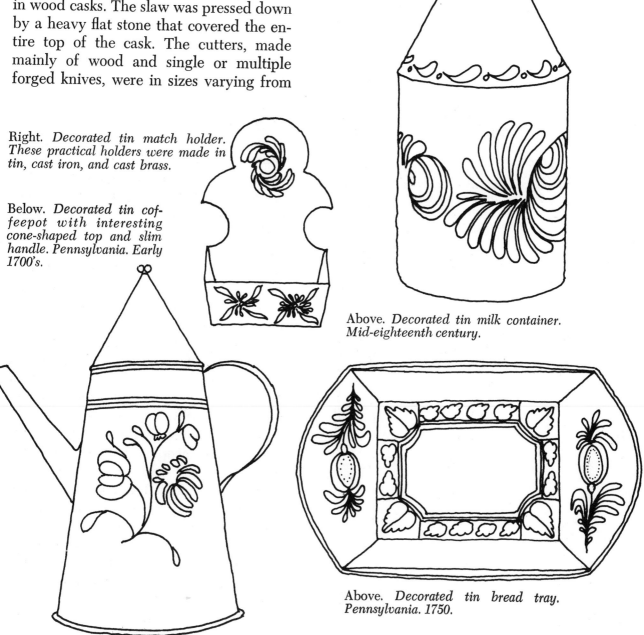

Right. *Decorated tin match holder. These practical holders were made in tin, cast iron, and cast brass.*

Below. *Decorated tin coffeepot with interesting cone-shaped top and slim handle. Pennsylvania. Early 1700's.*

Above. *Decorated tin milk container. Mid-eighteenth century.*

Above. *Decorated tin bread tray. Pennsylvania. 1750.*

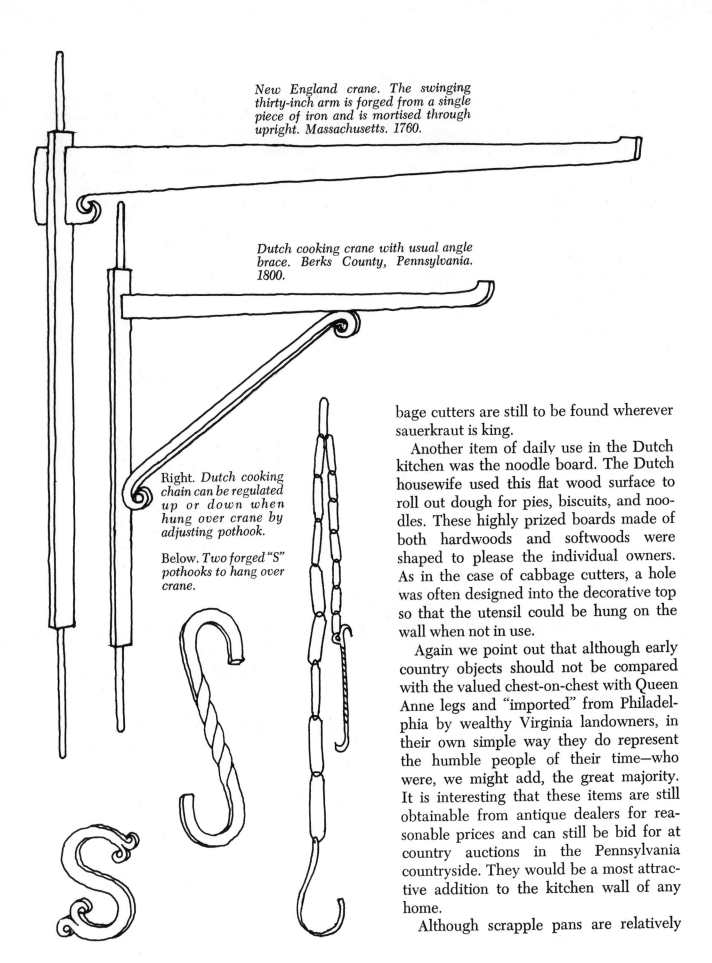

New England crane. The swinging thirty-inch arm is forged from a single piece of iron and is mortised through upright. Massachusetts. 1760.

Dutch cooking crane with usual angle brace. Berks County, Pennsylvania. 1800.

Right. *Dutch cooking chain can be regulated up or down when hung over crane by adjusting pothook.*

Below. *Two forged "S" pothooks to hang over crane.*

bage cutters are still to be found wherever sauerkraut is king.

Another item of daily use in the Dutch kitchen was the noodle board. The Dutch housewife used this flat wood surface to roll out dough for pies, biscuits, and noodles. These highly prized boards made of both hardwoods and softwoods were shaped to please the individual owners. As in the case of cabbage cutters, a hole was often designed into the decorative top so that the utensil could be hung on the wall when not in use.

Again we point out that although early country objects should not be compared with the valued chest-on-chest with Queen Anne legs and "imported" from Philadelphia by wealthy Virginia landowners, in their own simple way they do represent the humble people of their time—who were, we might add, the great majority. It is interesting that these items are still obtainable from antique dealers for reasonable prices and can still be bid for at country auctions in the Pennsylvania countryside. They would be a most attractive addition to the kitchen wall of any home.

Although scrapple pans are relatively

modern, the later sheet-iron type, dating from 1900, is made in simple black oval shapes that add a decorative note to the wall that is almost "contemporary modern" in design. It must be remembered that 1900 was only seventy years ago, clearly pointing up the fact that American antiques are, in a manner of speaking, self-replenishing.

When we suggest the use of wagon seats or a broommaker's bench to furnish a terrace or porch or, indeed, a country living

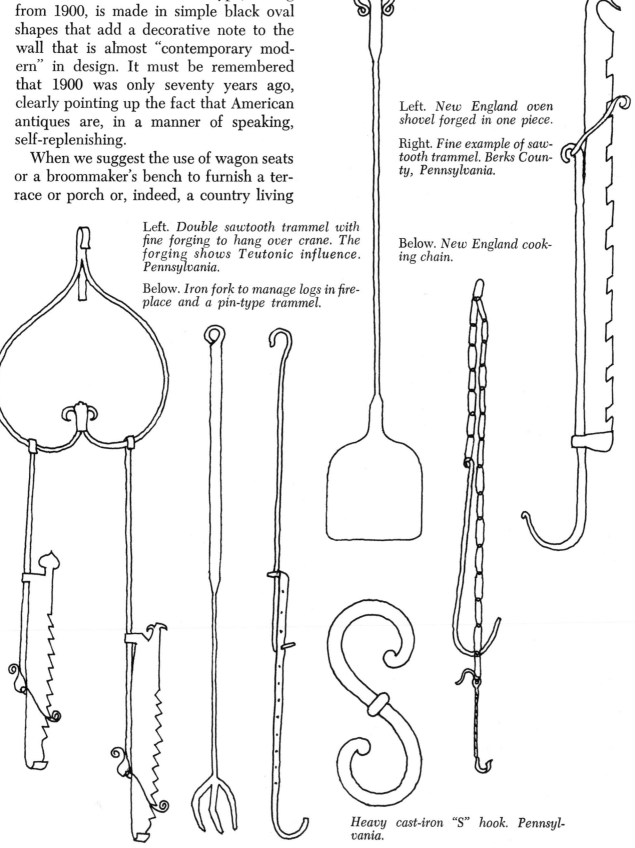

Left. *Double sawtooth trammel with fine forging to hang over crane. The forging shows Teutonic influence. Pennsylvania.*

Below. *Iron fork to manage logs in fireplace and a pin-type trammel.*

Left. *New England oven shovel forged in one piece.*

Right. *Fine example of sawtooth trammel. Berks County, Pennsylvania.*

Below. *New England cooking chain.*

Heavy cast-iron "S" hook. Pennsylvania.

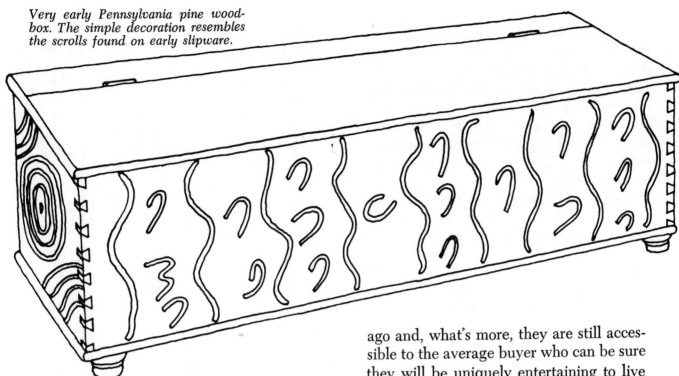

Very early Pennsylvania pine wood-box. The simple decoration resembles the scrolls found on early slipware.

room, we know we are in trouble with some collectors; but everyone cannot have pieces that are best displayed and appreciated from across a velvet rope in reputable museums. These unnamed and unsung pieces are as American as the people who used them over one hundred years ago and, what's more, they are still accessible to the average buyer who can be sure they will be uniquely entertaining to live with.

One may get the impression that we are suggesting you furnish your home with improvised bits and parts of colonial objects that were made for anything other than the use to which we wish to put them. This isn't really so; we only desire

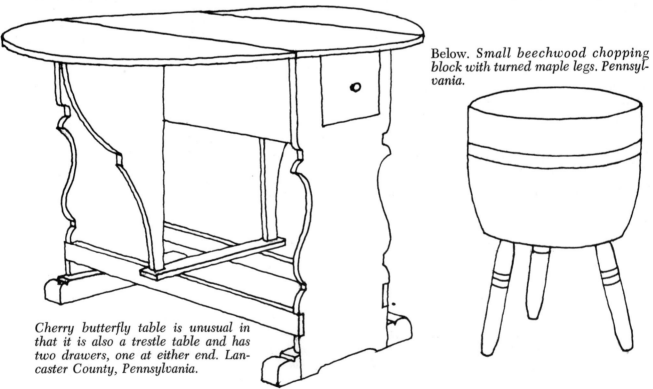

Cherry butterfly table is unusual in that it is also a trestle table and has two drawers, one at either end. Lancaster County, Pennsylvania.

Below. *Small beechwood chopping block with turned maple legs. Pennsylvania.*

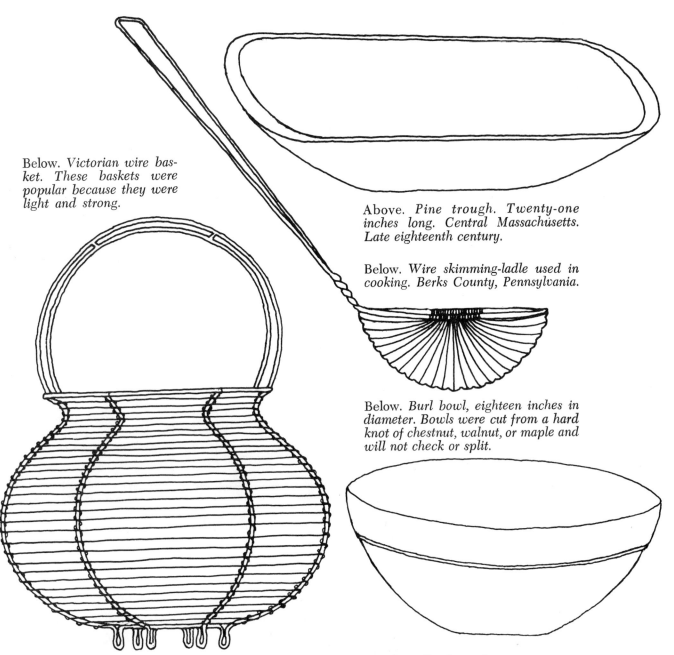

Below. *Victorian wire basket. These baskets were popular because they were light and strong.*

Above. *Pine trough. Twenty-one inches long. Central Massachusetts. Late eighteenth century.*

Below. *Wire skimming-ladle used in cooking. Berks County, Pennsylvania.*

Below. *Burl bowl, eighteen inches in diameter. Bowls were cut from a hard knot of chestnut, walnut, or maple and will not check or split.*

to convey what a very important part imagination plays in decisions to purchase.

If we give you any ideas that help you see how antiques can fit into your way of life, we have accomplished our purpose. Often newly interested collectors are hesitant about buying a piece they want because they have no specific need for it. We are not telling you to be extravagant, but as longtime collectors we know that you will probably join the long list of people who could kick themselves for not having

purchased when the opportunity presented itself. You will probably never see the same antique for the same price again.

If we sound preoccupied with collecting some of the lesser-known and less expensive antiques, it is because we know that as you learn you will eventually improve your collection. We have never known anyone who, once he had started collecting Americana, didn't steadily better the quality and value of his collection as time went on.

Because antiques are self-replenishing,

Above. *Decorated turned-wood egg-cup. Pennsylvania. Eighteenth century.*

it is practically impossible to do an exhaustive study on the subject. After collating the massive amount of material on antiques, we can only hope to cover enough to interest you in the subject as a whole. If you are planning to study this subject in depth, we must warn you that in Pennsylvania alone there are estimated to be thousands of varieties of cupboards.

We hope we will be able to provoke

Below. *Dough tray used for bread-making. The cover, when inverted, became a kneading board.*

Pennsylvania dry sink with breadboard top. Pine. Nineteenth century.

some recognition of the unsung antiques of our history, for their individual designs and excellent workmanship make them extremely desirable to own. It only takes the initiative of an interested person. Per-

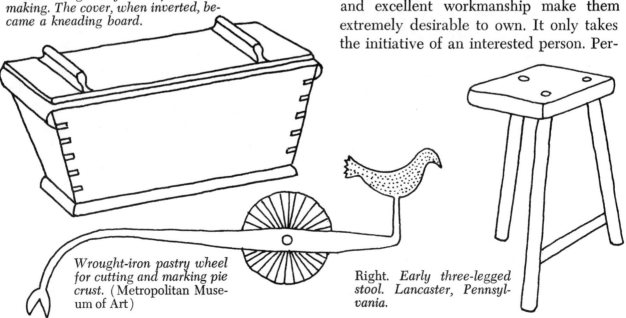

Wrought-iron pastry wheel for cutting and marking pie crust. (Metropolitan Museum of Art)

Right. *Early three-legged stool. Lancaster, Pennsylvania.*

Right. *Covered redware jar with slip decoration. Pennsylvania. Eighteenth century.*

Below. *Bennington teapot. New England. Eighteenth century.*

Right. *Primitive pine butter scoop. New England.*

Below. *Painted Pennsylvania dough trough. Dauphin County. 1780–1800.*

haps some inspiration may be provided by our own ways of decorating with these historical pieces and by showing you, in the photographs, how attractive they are and how easy to live with they can be. They are authentic American antiques even if their makers' names may never be known.

Most present-day collectors know that it is in this relatively unexplored category of antiques that the greatest opportunities lie. It is here that the newly interested collector can find furnishings and decorative objects with history and charm to start his collection. In this imaginative area, American antiques are still available and accessible in price. Perhaps as time goes on, they will, by virtue of their very honesty of design and construction, take their proper place with the established

Punched tin pie safe. Berks County, Pennsylvania. 1800.

and recognized classics of American antiques.

Pewter was used in great quantities during the settling of the Colonies. As the economic conditions improved and households became the storehouses of more luxuries, pewter was abandoned for silver. However, pewter did remain in use in the more modest homes until it was finally replaced by the less expensive earthenware that was to follow.

Although pewter in the home became less and less utilitarian, its handsome texture and color made it useful for decorative purposes. Public places like inns and taverns, where pewter remained in use much longer because of its practicality, were the last to convert to earthenware. But these same places took great pride in their old pewter mugs and plates and displayed them long after earthenware became acceptable and popular. This probably accounts for the quantity of common pewter that is still available. The plates with simple, broad, flat rims are still most attractive and effective for interior decorating. Bowls, teapots, and tankards may still be found in shops and purchased through dealers.

Perhaps the most appealing qualities of pewter are its modestly subdued sheen and its satisfyingly substantial weight. Most of the artisans of this metal were Englishmen who had settled in New York and began making pewter pieces to order as early as 1744.

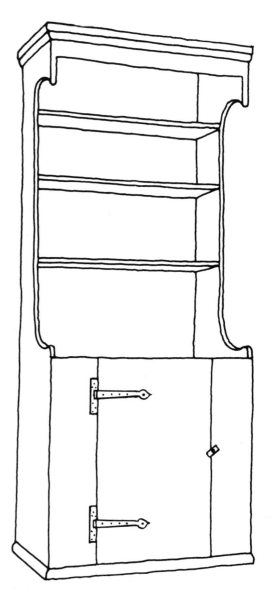

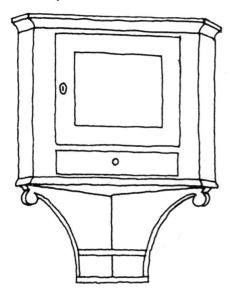

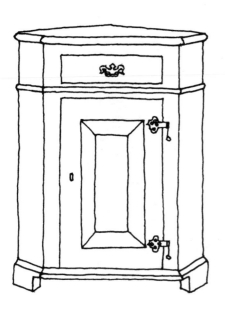

Left. *Pennsylvania corner cupboards were most effective when arranged one above the other. The hinges on the base are a later adaptation of the early rattail. 1820–1840.*

Above right. *Open pine cupboard with covered end boards and short arrowhead hinges. New England. Eighteenth century.*

Right. *Bench table, the top of which can be swung back to form a bench. Wooden pins serve as hinges. It was sometimes used for a seat near a fireplace because the high back reflected heat and prevented draughts.*

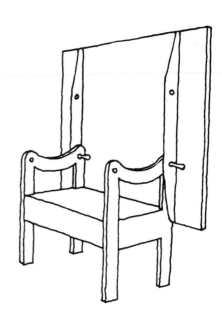

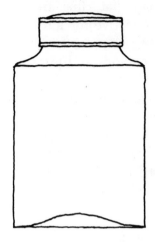

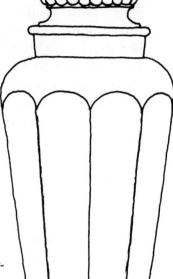

Three early blown-glass storage jars with tin covers.

Right. *Late Victorian storage jar or candy jar.*

There were many variations in the basic composition of pewter. The formulas were influenced by the areas in which it was produced and by the purpose for which each piece was to be ultimately used.

Price and quality also influenced the formulation. The best quality plate pewter was made up of eighty-eight parts tin to which were added eight parts antimony and four parts copper. The more common pewter had eighteen parts antimony to eighty-two parts tin, and no copper. Pipe metal was sixty parts tin and forty parts lead with no copper or antimony. It was

Painted tin tray. New England. Nineteenth century.

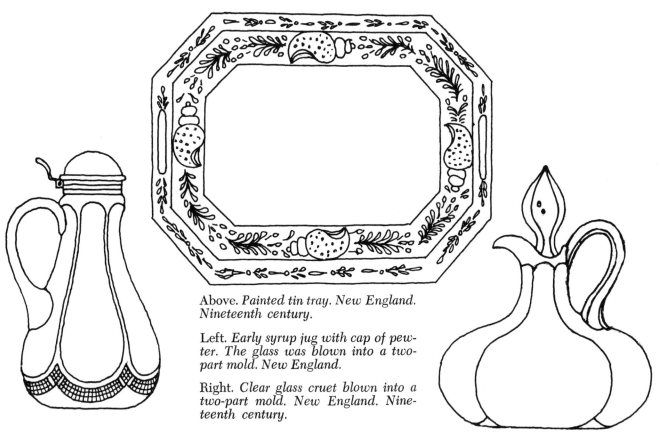

Above. *Painted tin tray. New England. Nineteenth century.*

Left. *Early syrup jug with cap of pewter. The glass was blown into a two-part mold. New England.*

Right. *Clear glass cruet blown into a two-part mold. New England. Nineteenth century.*

occasionally sold as pewter to the unsuspecting. Tin, the bulk ingredient in pewter, is recorded to have been in use in Egypt before 3500 B.C. It was used in combination with copper.

The earliest English pewtermakers drew their basic metals, tin and lead, from the productive Cornish mines that had supplied Rome, Holland, Spain, and France for centuries. Documents of the prolific trade in these metals date as early as the thirteenth century. History tells us that in the middle 1500's, François Briot of France was one of the better-known

Pressed-glass rooster-and-hen covered dishes were made of gilded clear glass, frosted glass, and opaque milk glass. Early Victorian.

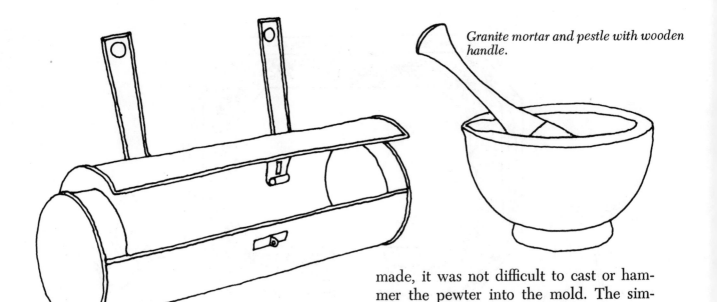

Granite mortar and pestle with wooden handle.

Tin candle holder with sturdy straps for hanging. The hasp is the simple type commonly used by tinsmiths. 1810–1850.

makers of objects in this soft metal. The art spread to other parts of Europe, and became most important in Switzerland and Germany.

In England, each pewterer had a private mark. Each master had two marks, the larger seal designed from the first letter of his Christian name and his entire surname, the smaller one holding only the initials of both his names.

The easily worked metal took the place of household utensils made of wood. Once a mold of hard wood or gun metal was

Wrought-iron whirling broiler, with hooked handle and straight design.

made, it was not difficult to cast or hammer the pewter into the mold. The simpler burnishing or brightening of the molded objects was usually done by apprentices; it was very desirable for young men to apprentice into this booming and seemingly everlasting trade.

In colonial days, pewter was very important in the making of candle molds. Pewter forms were used to mold tallow candles, the only source of light other than the early oil lamps of the same period. An excerpt from Francis Higginson's writings in 1630 mentions that New Eng-

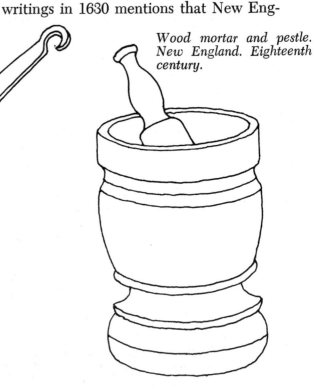

Wood mortar and pestle. New England. Eighteenth century.

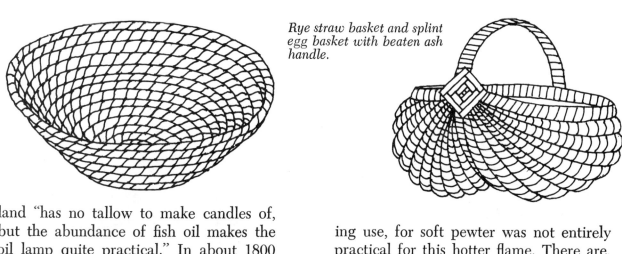

Rye straw basket and splint egg basket with beaten ash handle.

land "has no tallow to make candles of, but the abundance of fish oil makes the oil lamp quite practical." In about 1800 it is recorded that liquid bitumin (petroleum) was found oozing through fissures in coal and floating in rainwater pools or springs and was discovered to be extremely flammable. This compelled a change in metal work for lamp or light-

ing use, for soft pewter was not entirely practical for this hotter flame. There are, however, some very early pewter lamps made for petroleum; one in Washington, D.C., is said to have come from Mount Vernon and was supposedly in use at the time of George Washington. Although the most common pieces of pewter were made for utilitarian and domestic use, they also took other forms. In 1729 the First Church of Hanover, Massachusetts, bought a set of communion vessels and a christening basin all made of pewter. There are also

Left. *Rye straw basket made of heavy spiral twists of straw woven together with narrow strips of hickory. Baskets of this type were used to store dried fruit.*

Left. *Very early spider or pan for the fireplace. Legs and long handle are integral parts of this cooking utensil.*

Right. *Wrought-iron whirling broiler with serpentine forgings.*

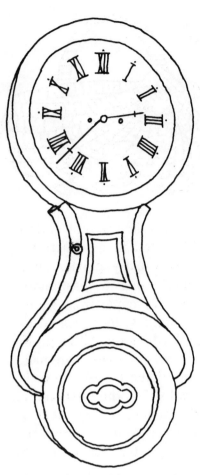

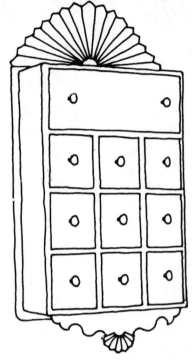

Right. *Aaron Willard wall regulator clock with single-panel door.*

Below. *Hanging spice cupboard with large and small sunburst decorations. Eighteenth century.*

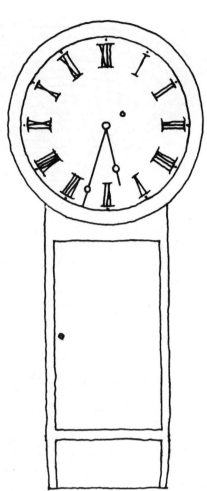

Wall regulator clock with striking banjo movement. George D. Hatch, North Attleboro, Massachusetts. 1850.

many records of the great value people attached to objects made of pewter in early wills, settlements, or estates, and in the books of shops dealing in metal objects. People spoke of this highly prized material in the same terms that silver enjoyed at a later date.

The earliest colonial pewter was lost forever during the Revolutionary War. At that time, pewter not absolutely necessary for important daily functions was given up and made into bullets by and for the patriots.

If we were to take up the subject of scales, there would be room for little else in this book, for the variety of needs, uses, materials, and manufacturers matches that of clocks. Indeed, scales did predate clocks, though perhaps not sundials. After all,

weighing something can be as primitive as "hefting" an object in one's hand. "Bailing" scales were simple balance arms and were forged and in use in the earliest colonial farms and even before. As people became more selective about their purchases and bought smaller amounts at a time, smaller and more delicate scales were needed. The balance scale, still basically the most accurate, was constructed simply of an arm and two equally balanced platforms, one to hold the item to be weighed and the other to hold the measured weight. These were cast, decorated, and sold throughout the Colonies until "named" manufacturers took over the "honest weight" business early in the nineteenth century. Incidentally, some of these early manufacturers' names are still most prominent in this field, but the prod-

Below. *Primitive hanging corner cupboard with beveled panels on door, iron strap hinges, tiny quarter-round shelf set into scrolled sides.*

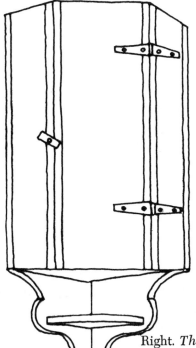

Above. *Shelf clock. N. L. Brewster and Company, Bristol, Connecticut. 1861.*

Above right. *Hanging cupboard with double-paneled door, unusual scrolled heart at top. Early nineteenth century.*

Right. *The Connecticut wall regulator was a very good timepiece. Thousands of these popular clocks were made right up to the beginning of the twentieth century.*

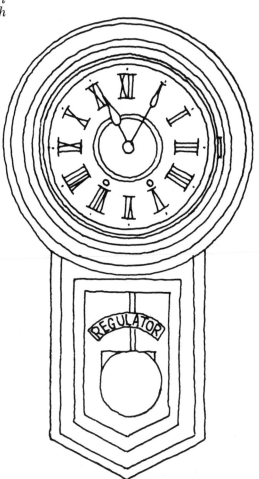

ucts they make are by no means as simple as they once were, though they are certainly more accurate.

Wirework became very popular in the early nineteenth century when new methods of drawing thinner wire opened the field of manufacturing wire utensils. Strong, light, and capable of performing many kitchen duties, these utensils became quite popular. Egg and potato wicker baskets were replaced by sturdy wire pieces, many of which are still being made for the same uses. The decorative wirework was used to embellish flow-blue dishes and bowls. These popular pieces, often commemorative in nature, were quite charming with their lacy fringe of wire. Picture frames that decorated homes in late Victorian times often had a fringe of this same wirework.

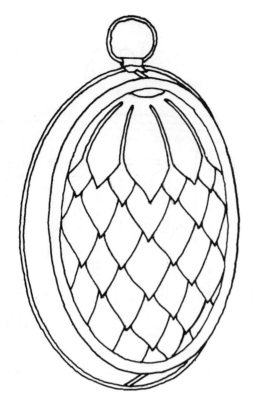

Above. *Heavy tin pineapple mold.
Berks County, Pennsylvania.*

Below. *Tin washbasin. Late nineteenth
century.*

Stiegel, the more enterprising of the two glassmakers, produced glass of both the soda-lime and the flint varieties. He produced all the basic necessities of those times as well as the decorative pieces that are now so sought after. Another important name in glassmaking in the 1790's was John Frederick Amelung, whose glassworks operated at Frederick, Maryland. His deeply engraved pieces of fine quality and superb workmanship were likened to the better Irish glass of the same period. The few pieces of Amelung that are in private collections and not in museums are deemed precious: Either Amelung was not a prolific manufacturer, or his pieces have been lost in use and time.

Because the finest early glass is difficult to find and is extremely expensive, we will move on to the subject of glass in early 1825, when the pressed glass which is still available to the collector began to

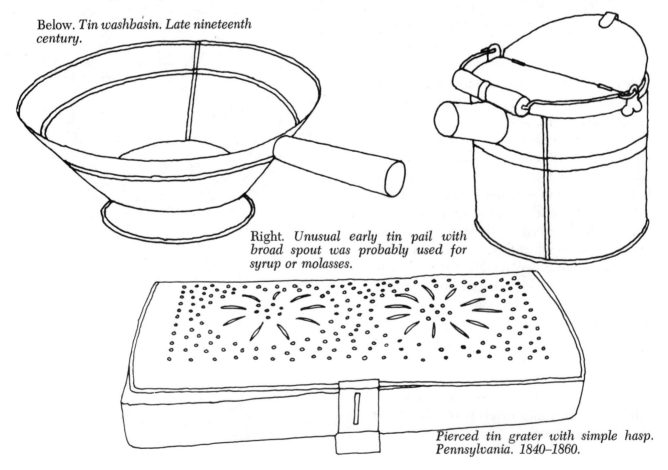

Right. *Unusual early tin pail with
broad spout was probably used for
syrup or molasses.*

*Pierced tin grater with simple hasp.
Pennsylvania. 1840–1860.*

126

come into its own. Once looked upon by collectors of means as an inferior product of glassmakers, time has made many of these attractive pieces highly desirable. When Dening Jarnes, a glassworker with the New England Glass Company, patented a press for more efficient glassmaking and joined with the Sandwich Company of Boston, volume production of pressed glass was on its way. Pressed glass was produced in more than fifteen factories in more than a thousand patterns, and a

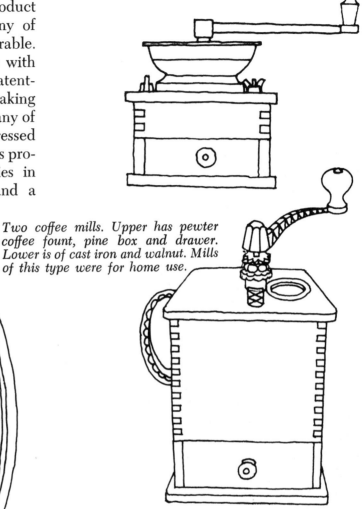

Two coffee mills. Upper has pewter coffee fount, pine box and drawer. Lower is of cast iron and walnut. Mills of this type were for home use.

Large cast-iron store coffee mill, decorated with brass eagle. 1870–1890.

variety of colors. Pressed glass in every imaginable shape and design, both decorative and utilitarian, was advertised, marketed, and enjoyed by everyone throughout the country, rich and poor alike.

Pressed glass, along with decorative and colorful blown and overlay pieces, is the category we are most interested in for the purposes of this book. These pieces are available, they are American antiques, they are interesting and, in many cases, quite beautiful, and, importantly, they will increase in value, for they are becoming highly acceptable to the most important collectors.

Charming tulip-ware pottery mugs, jugs,

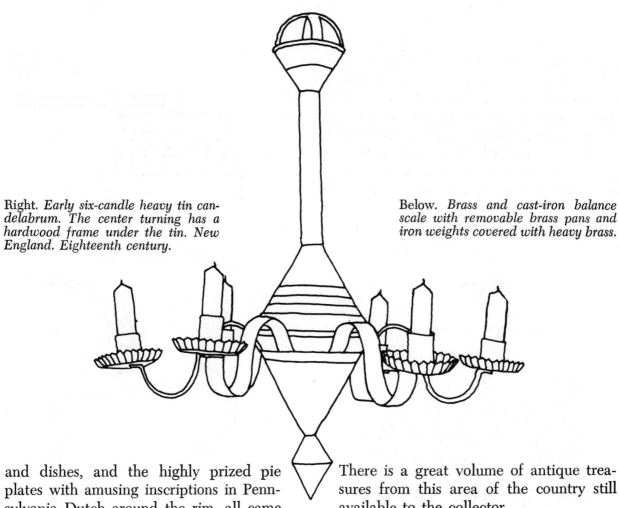

Right. *Early six-candle heavy tin candelabrum. The center turning has a hardwood frame under the tin. New England. Eighteenth century.*

Below. *Brass and cast-iron balance scale with removable brass pans and iron weights covered with heavy brass.*

and dishes, and the highly prized pie plates with amusing inscriptions in Pennsylvania Dutch around the rim, all came out of the same section of Pennsylvania at about the same time.

Early Pennsylvania Dutch peasant art manifested itself in the creation of beautiful and utilitarian pieces. The artisans of Pennsylvania were tireless workers and made quantities of sturdy objects that have withstood the test of time and use.

There is a great volume of antique treasures from this area of the country still available to the collector.

In the next chapter, which is devoted to antiques for use in the bedroom, we will discuss articles made of the same materials and by the same techniques as those in this chapter. We feel, however, that they are bedroom things and that is why we put them there. We hope you will agree with our choice.

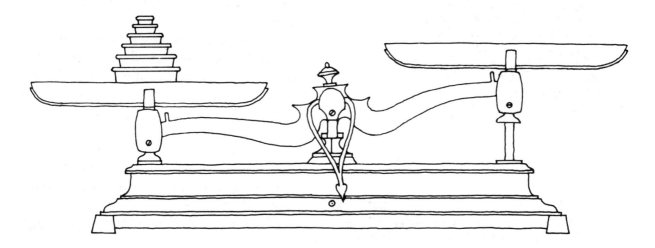

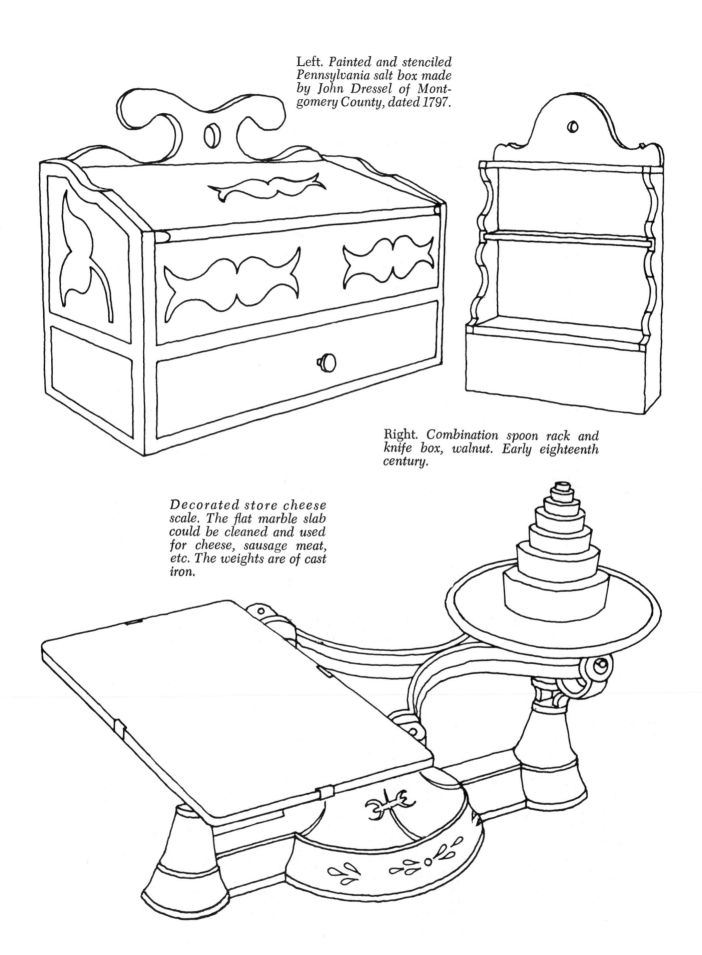

Left. *Painted and stenciled Pennsylvania salt box made by John Dressel of Montgomery County, dated 1797.*

Right. *Combination spoon rack and knife box, walnut. Early eighteenth century.*

Decorated store cheese scale. The flat marble slab could be cleaned and used for cheese, sausage meat, etc. The weights are of cast iron.

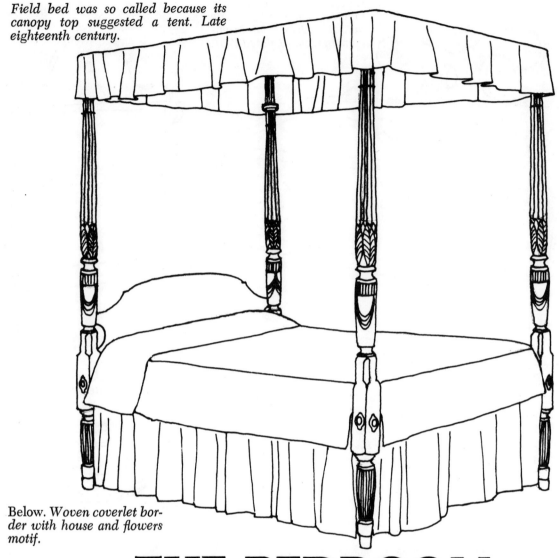

Field bed was so called because its canopy top suggested a tent. Late eighteenth century.

Below. *Woven coverlet border with house and flowers motif.*

THE BEDROOM

A bedroom is feminine. A bedroom is bright in the daytime, soft and quiet at night. A bedroom is where the lady of the house collects her most prized and intimate possessions. A bedroom is a canopy bed, quantities of colorful drapes, hand-worked spreads and linens, filmy things, and romantic bric-a-brac.

However, a bedroom was not always thought of in this poetic way. The settlers

Above. *Corner of woven coverlet showing maker's name.*

Below. *Urn with flowers motif was used in coverlet borders.*

Above. Woven coverlet with peacocks, turkeys and rosettes. Pennsylvania.

Below. *Coverlet motif showing bird on a branch.*

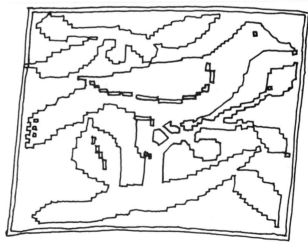

of our Colonies rested where they could after their long day's work. A special place for sleeping was not part of the primitive living plan. We do know, however, that eventually a room was set aside in the primitive house for this essential purpose. It became a retreat away from the activities and noises of the family, a newly assigned area that was a sanctuary expressly for sleeping. At first, it was just a corner of the room; later it became permanently positioned and named. The label "bedroom" was quite accurate, for originally all it contained was a bed. This small yet separated part of an early house,

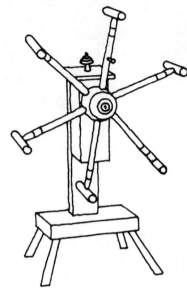

Below. *Pine reel. The length of the yarn is measured by the number of revolutions. A wood clapper in the box, activated by a worm gear, signals each revolution.*

Above. *Decorated four-poster bed with stippling and painted sunken panels. Pennsylvania Dutch.*

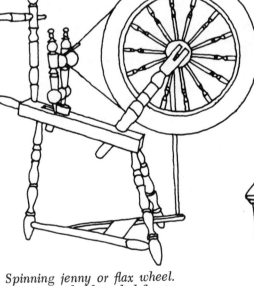

which now we cannot conceive of doing without, was slow to dignify itself as an important component on the list of house rooms.

The colonists labored from dawn to dusk and only when the time came to rest did they give a thought to the place where they slept. Just the most fundamental furnishings were needed, for it was in use only during the night. It was not important otherwise. That is, not until the woman of the house saw it as her private domain.

It was then and only then that the bedroom began to come into its own.

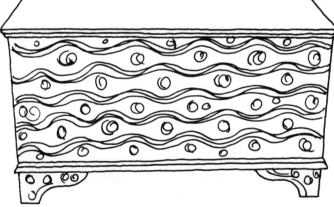

Above. *Spinning jenny or flax wheel. Bowed cage at top held carded flax to be spun into thread.*

Right. *Small blanket chest painted and boldly decorated with a dry brush. This type of decoration is sometimes called "feather painting."*

Since the bedroom was exclusively for sleeping, in those frugal times, the duplication of furnishings to decorate it would have been both wasteful and impractical. It is little wonder that it was the last room in the house to which any decorating thought was given. It did have a most important champion, however, in the lady of the house. Her interest and influence on the decor of this particular room did at last, and will forever, make the bedroom more of a woman's room than any other room in the house.

Since people do collect things about them and the homemaker's instinct is to make her home look ever better, the bedroom eventually began to take on a new look. It became a room instead of a corner of the main room; it won a door for privacy and enough space for some furnishings other than the bed. Of course, these furnishings had to be utilitarian; practically all furnishings for every part

Bobbin wheel was used to prepare the yarn for the loom. The thread was finished by additional twisting and stretching.

of the house had a useful purpose. Furnishings for the bedroom pertained to the bedroom: places for clothes and toilet articles, storage of bedding, and, of course, sleeping. It was because of this expansion of bedroom functions that the room began

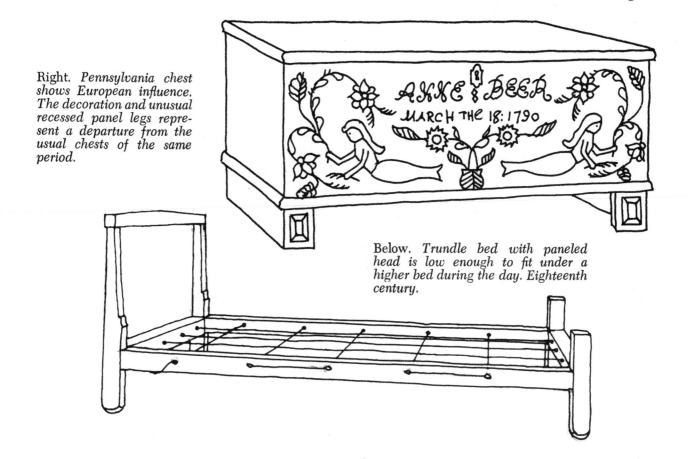

Right. *Pennsylvania chest shows European influence. The decoration and unusual recessed panel legs represent a departure from the usual chests of the same period.*

Below. *Trundle bed with paneled head is low enough to fit under a higher bed during the day. Eighteenth century.*

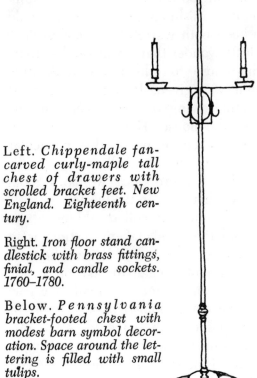

Left. *Chippendale fan-carved curly-maple tall chest of drawers with scrolled bracket feet. New England. Eighteenth century.*

Right. *Iron floor stand candlestick with brass fittings, finial, and candle sockets. 1760–1780.*

Below. *Pennsylvania bracket-footed chest with modest barn symbol decoration. Space around the lettering is filled with small tulips.*

to take its rightful place as an attractive as well as important addition to the house.

Heating the newly appointed room was not even considered; people didn't need heat just for sleeping and besides wasting fuel was akin to sinfulness. Only in the townhouses or the country homes of the "landed" people did the bedroom enjoy its own fireplace or stove. In the country areas the activity of retiring was accomplished in a dash from the warmth of the kitchen fire into the covers on the bed

William and Mary tall chest of drawers with curly-maple drawer fronts and bulbous feet was made in the Housatonic Valley of Connecticut between 1690 and 1720.

in the frigid room. Not until late in the nineteenth century did people begin to keep the bedroom as warm as the rest of the house. Indeed, some still believe it more healthful to sleep in a cold room. We are happy that this idea is now optional.

One of the first of the useful pieces that became a standard bedroom furnishing was the chest. The chest, often used as a trunk for transporting clothes and bedding, was quite a useful piece of furniture for the sleeping area. However, it did not retain its simple finish or construction for long. Its usage was expanded by adding drawers for items of daily use and it was reclassified a chest with drawers. Later, the top chest part was eliminated,

135

Below. *An ear of corn is the decorative motif on this octagonal Empire drawer pull. 1810.*

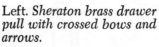

Left. *Sheraton brass drawer pull with crossed bows and arrows.*

Right. *Hepplewhite bow-front chest of drawers with dressing mirror. The mirror was not constructed as a permanent part of the chest.*

but what remained was still called a "chest of drawers." The chest part returned to its single and original function as a place to store things, and so we now had three specific functional furnishings for the bedroom: a bed, a chest, and a chest of drawers. The large wooden chests performed a double duty. First, they were used to store bedding and clothing not in daily use; second, they were usually placed at the foot of the bed and used as a bench to be sat on. This was the origin of the foot locker. In any case, the chest became an item of singular importance, often made of the best materials by the finest of cabinetmakers, sometimes banded with fine forgings of iron or brass, with intricate locks to secure the cherished items it held. In Pennsylvania and New England, these chests were often beautifully decorated and became the single most important article of furniture for the unmarried daughter of the house. It was in these dower chests that she collected the linens and quilts and personal things that she would use in her new life when she married.

Originally the bedroom was anything but an attractive room. Wooden pegs were driven into the wall near the bed to hold the day-to-day clothes. Of course, there was little need for a special place to store

Chippendale walnut chest of drawers with brass fittings and ogee feet.

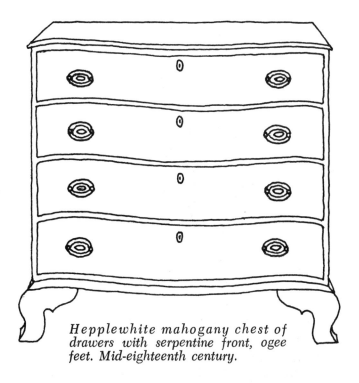

Hepplewhite mahogany chest of drawers with serpentine front, ogee feet. Mid-eighteenth century.

clothes when people had few extra garments. If there was a lamp in the bedroom, it was undoubtedly one borrowed from the living area of the house. Certainly few of the early colonists could afford the extra fuel or, indeed, an extra lamp.

It was not until the development of glass lamps that bedroom decorating really was started in earnest. A lamp the bedroom could call its very own suddenly made that room pleasantly habitable after dark. The lamp, of course, needed to rest on something steady, and so a bed table was added to the essential furnishings. The light of the lamp now called attention to the clothes hanging from the wall pegs and casting eerie shadows on the wall. This was sufficient to make the housewife see the need of a closet or *kas* in which to store clothes. Certainly,

Above. *Sheraton brass drawer pull with solid brass twisted spiral or rope motif handle.*

Left. *Mirror with handsome mahogany frame is in the Queen Anne style of the 1700's.*

Right. *An attractive American Chippendale mirror of mahogany, with fine scrollwork.*

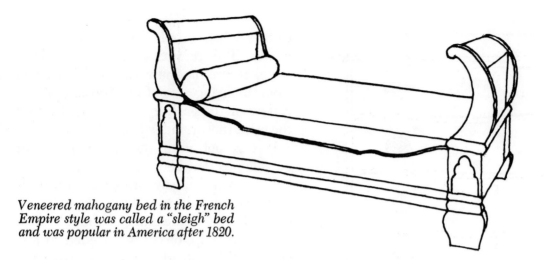

Veneered mahogany bed in the French Empire style was called a "sleigh" bed and was popular in America after 1820.

this additional bedroom furnishing was a practical as well as a decorative improvement.

When the clothes pegs were removed from the bedroom walls and replaced by the closet, all the essential bedroom furnishings were accounted for. It now only remained to improve the individual func-

tions of these furnishings and to beautify their design and construction. The huge cabinets—or *kases*, as they were called in Pennsylvania—were made with excellent workmanship with fine wood. Forerunners of the built-in closet, they performed their duties until the late nineteenth century when architects began to design closets

Below. *A very early drawer pull of solid brass, probably from New England.*

Below. *Stamped brass drawer pull. Late eighteenth century.*

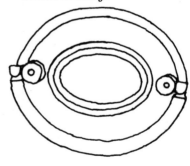

Left. *Queen Anne tall chest-of-drawers. The short cabriole legs and base molding are very similar to the separate frame sometimes used in the same period. This piece is typical of early New England cabinet work. 1735–1760.*

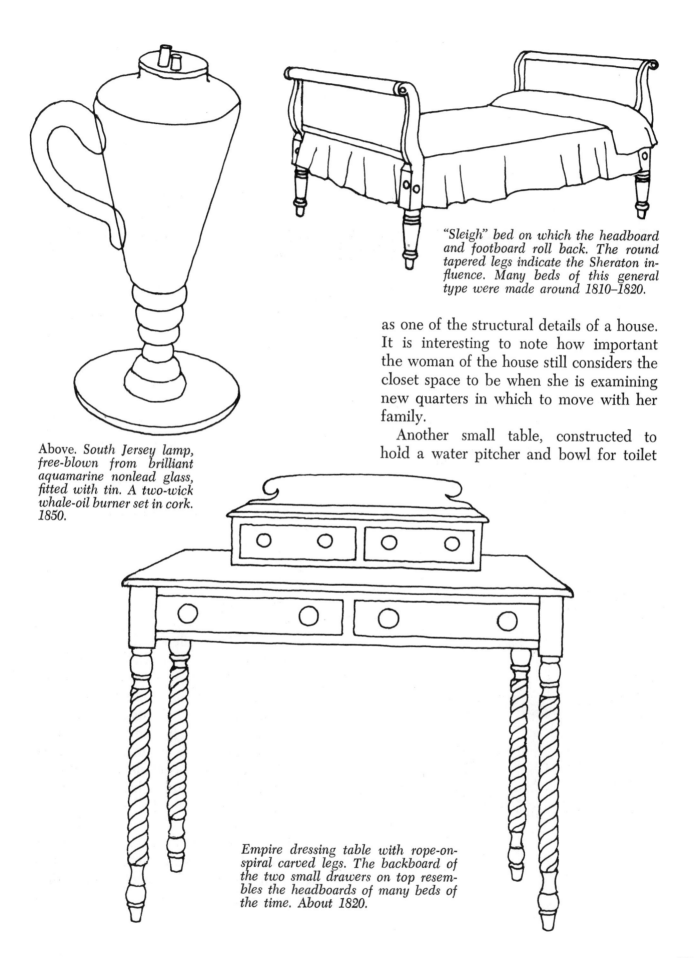

"Sleigh" bed on which the headboard and footboard roll back. The round tapered legs indicate the Sheraton influence. Many beds of this general type were made around 1810–1820.

Above. South Jersey lamp, free-blown from brilliant aquamarine nonlead glass, fitted with tin. A two-wick whale-oil burner set in cork. 1850.

as one of the structural details of a house. It is interesting to note how important the woman of the house still considers the closet space to be when she is examining new quarters in which to move with her family.

Another small table, constructed to hold a water pitcher and bowl for toilet

Empire dressing table with rope-on-spiral carved legs. The backboard of the two small drawers on top resembles the headboards of many beds of the time. About 1820.

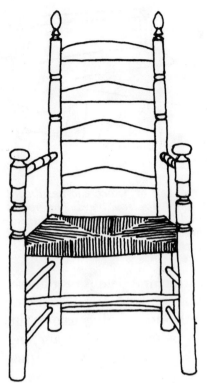

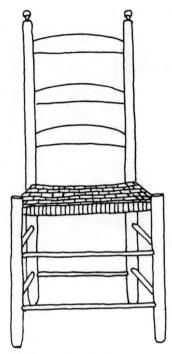

Turned maple and hickory "Carver
arhchair" has sausage-turned uprights
with acorn finials, front posts with
mushroom finials, and double-stretch-
ered legs. New England. 1700.

Early eighteenth century
slat-back chair, with beaten
ash seat and mushroom finials.

Late arrow-back Windsor
rocker was the most pop-
ular style before the ad-
vent of the Boston rocker.

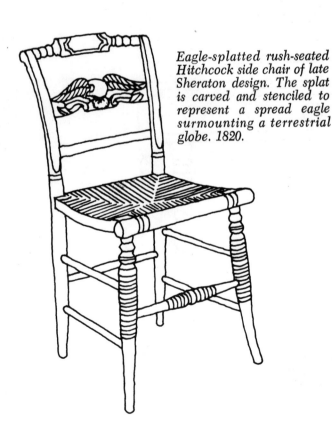

Eagle-splatted rush-seated
Hitchcock side chair of late
Sheraton design. The splat
is carved and stenciled to
represent a spread eagle
surmounting a terrestrial
globe. 1820.

use, was soon to be added to the bedroom.
In some cases this washstand had towel
racks on each side of its top and a shelf
at the bottom to hold the required china
chamber pot. In the homes of the more
finicky housewives of a later period, the
lid of the chamber pot was sure to be
covered by a crocheted cap that tucked
under the lid to silence the action of re-
turning it to the pot. Called "hushers,"
these delicate pieces of crocheted handiwork were a must in the bedrooms of the
most fastidious early Victorians.

As the bedroom became a more usual
place to spend some of the daylight hours,
articles began to be made especially for
use there. Lamps and lighting accessories
specially designed for bedrooms were introduced by enterprising manufacturers.
Colorful glass shades were hand-painted
or covered with decal transfers more delicate in color and subject matter than
those found on the all-purpose lamps in the

Above. *The Victorian chest of drawers is typical of the painted furniture period. The craftsman who painted this fruitwood chest in a bird's-eye maple design spent much time and care with the literally thousands of eyes each complete with a pupil. Pennsylvania Dutch. Reading.*

Below. *Pennsylvania four-poster with turned tulip design has a feather-painted back. The extra cuttings in the rolling pin on the top of the backboard indicate the period. The eagle pattern woven into the homespun cover and its bright color make it an excellent example of the folk art of early Pennsylvania.*

Above. *Very fine early pine Pennsylvania-Dutch kas, with elegant primitive painting.*

Below. *Early pine dressing table with late Victorian cast-iron mirror. In front of the bull's-eye bottles is a blue dish with wirework, late Victorian. The green lamp base is pressed glass.*

Left. *Dutch low-poster with early feather painting. Homespun quilt is dated 1840.*

Above. *Philadelphia mahogany highboy. Fine mahogany desk with several sets of tiny drawers on the inside, and rope legs. Early Victorian chairs. A dated sampler is over the desk. (Edwin F. Nimmo Collection, Barto, Pennsylvania)*

Below. *Iron and brass Victorian bed. The patchwork cover is Pennsylvania Dutch, 1870. Three-drawer maple and pine end table is a Berks County piece. On the far right is an unusual blue milk-glass top on a Dutch end table, origin unknown.*

living room. Butterflies and wild flowers, so attractive to women, were especially popular motifs. The hollow glass pedestals that supported the kerosene fount on standing lamps were made colorful with bright glass overlays or, if transparent, were filled with dried straw flowers or grain bouquets. In any case, bedroom decorating was beginning to come into its own. The woman of the house had a personal and private room and she intended to fill it with the things she liked.

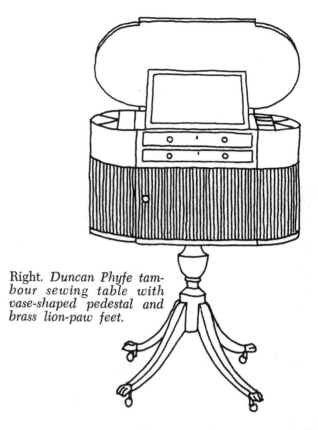

Right. *Duncan Phyfe tambour sewing table with vase-shaped pedestal and brass lion-paw feet.*

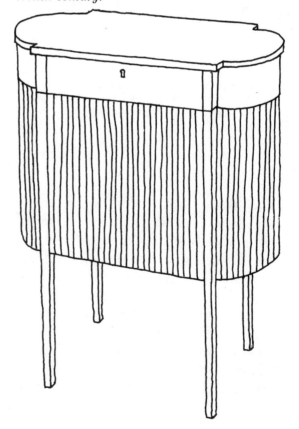

Below. *Sheraton lady's work table. The lower portions of the table are covered with pleated silk. Late eighteenth century.*

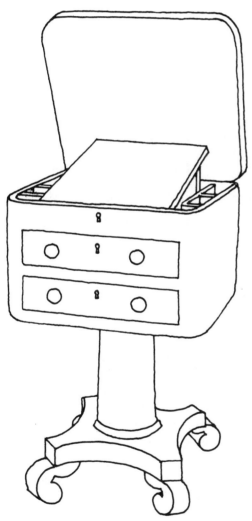

Late Empire style mahogany table, made about 1840. The top lifts up to provide a slanted writing board with small compartments on each side. This belonged to General Robert E. Lee and was used by him at Arlington and at Washington and Lee University where he was president.

Country washstand found in Waterloo, New York, was painted and decorated freehand, rather than stenciled, as was usual.

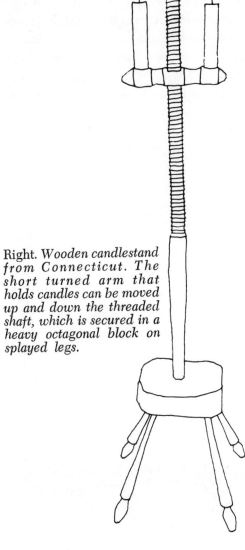

Right. Wooden candlestand from Connecticut. The short turned arm that holds candles can be moved up and down the threaded shaft, which is secured in a heavy octagonal block on splayed legs.

The coarse and colorless homespun covers, some thick with feathers or combed wool, gradually gave way to colorful and prized loomed wool homespun. The maker customarily wove in his name and the date so the cover carried a permanent bit of advertising for as long as it lasted. These beautifully designed and executed homespuns were covered with bright, colorful symbols typical of the times: patriotic eagles, Dutch country tulips, hearts, and other motifs, and the geometric designs so often seen in the equally early fractur.

Patchwork quilts, whose rather formalized basic geometric designs were carefully followed by most of the makers, can still be found at auctions and antique shops. The designs of these quilts were seldom changed but the choice of colors and materials used was left to the quilter's artistic taste and discretion. Often these attractive and beautifully made covers were a cherished part of the bride's dowry and, indeed, the quantity of early ones still available proves how carefully the quilts were treasured and cared for by their original owners.

Appliqué, a freer form of quilting, permitted the maker more artistic expression, and the decorative covers were an admirable way to display the handiwork and artistry of the lady or ladies of the house. These beautiful representations of this primitive American folk art are difficult to come by, for the cotton materials were quite fragile and suffered from constant use. Quilting was often a communal project and groups of women joined together to share work and socialize.

To learn the origin of canopy beds, it is necessary to go back to medieval times. During that period canopy beds found great favor among people of wealth and power. The canopy bed was certainly designed for privacy: The head and footboards were high-paneled and, when the side curtains were dropped, the bed was a room unto itself. Frequently it had a solid wood ceiling rather than the more familiar woven material covering the top. Night air was something to be feared in

Mid-nineteenth century balloon-back chair with plank seat of poplar was designed for comfort. The round back and spindles are of maple or hickory. These chairs were painted, varnished, and decorated with stencils in popular motifs of the day.

those times and the ability to close oneself in was a protection against that. It also created an area small enough to be easily warmed. Today, the purely decorative possibilities of these attractive and functional furnishings make the canopy

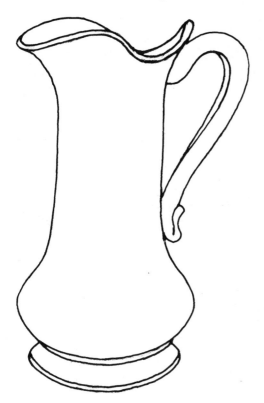

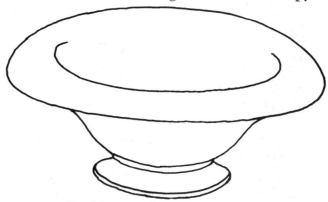

Hand basin and ewer of opaque white glass were probably blown in the glass house of Whitall Brothers who acquired the first glassworks built in Millville, New Jersey, in 1844.

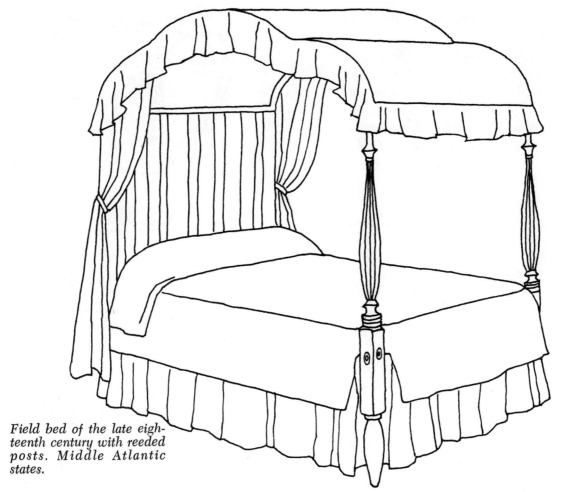

*Field bed of the late eigh-
teenth century with reeded
posts. Middle Atlantic
states.*

bed eagerly sought after by the collector
who lives with his American antiques.

Of all the furnishings designed for daily
use, now as well as then, the bed must be
constructed to carry more live weight than
any other piece of furniture in the house.
Up until the nineteenth century, with the
advent of the twin bed, beds were custom-

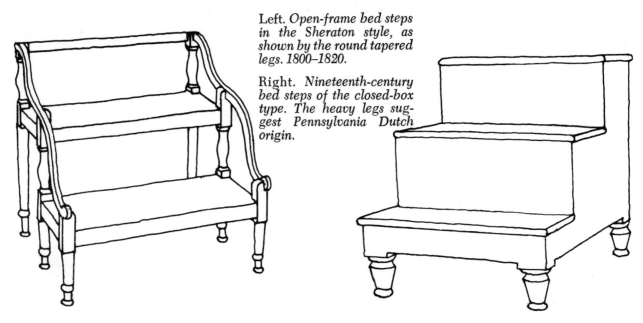

Left. *Open-frame bed steps
in the Sheraton style, as
shown by the round tapered
legs. 1800–1820.*

Right. *Nineteenth-century
bed steps of the closed-box
type. The heavy legs sug-
gest Pennsylvania Dutch
origin.*

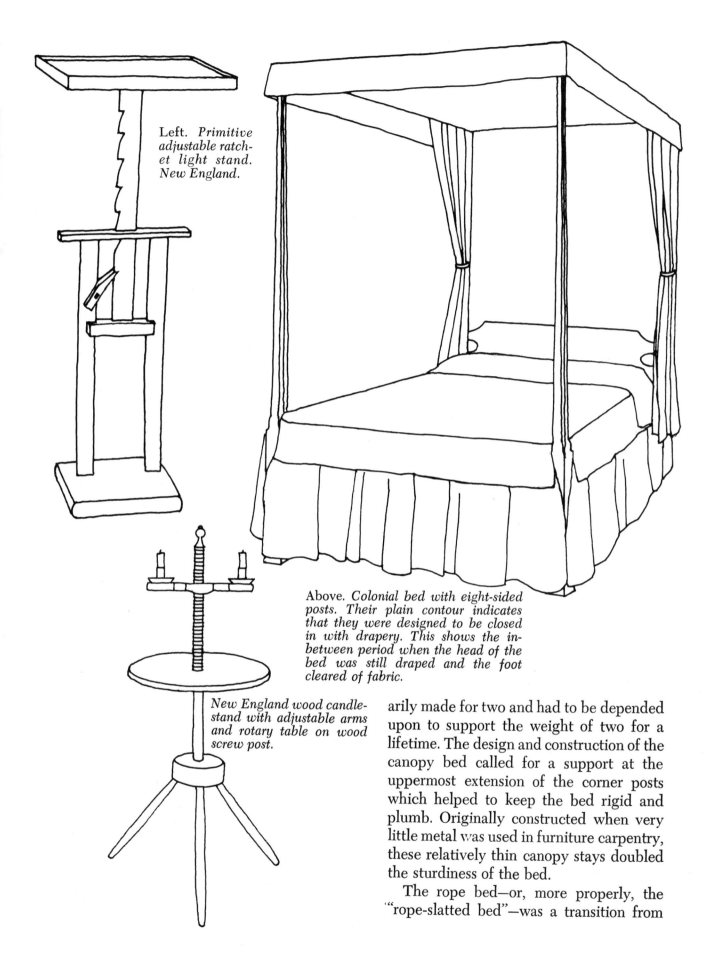

Left. *Primitive adjustable ratchet light stand. New England.*

Above. *Colonial bed with eight-sided posts. Their plain contour indicates that they were designed to be closed in with drapery. This shows the in-between period when the head of the bed was still draped and the foot cleared of fabric.*

New England wood candlestand with adjustable arms and rotary table on wood screw post.

arily made for two and had to be depended upon to support the weight of two for a lifetime. The design and construction of the canopy bed called for a support at the uppermost extension of the corner posts which helped to keep the bed rigid and plumb. Originally constructed when very little metal was used in furniture carpentry, these relatively thin canopy stays doubled the sturdiness of the bed.

The rope bed—or, more properly, the "rope-slatted bed"—was a transition from the wood-slatted bed to the solid spring bed. When a rope was laced either through the holes provided by the cabinetmaker or laced around the wood "buttons" set in the frame of the bed for this same purpose, it formed a springy web of support for the mattress.

On beds with left and right side rails, the rails were also threaded so that the

Hepplewhite chest of drawers with cupboard top, cast-brass eagle finial, and stamped-brass pulls.

Above. *This huge wardrobe or Pennsylvania Dutch* schrank *was used for storing clothes. Closets were nonexistent in early houses.*

Above. *Chippendale brass with plain surface, a popular pattern found on furniture made between 1760 and 1775.*

Late eighteenth-century stamped-brass pull with popular eagle motif.

weight of a body on the rope webbing would tighten the bed joinings. In any case, the ropes tended to stretch and, with time and use, sagged into a modified hammock shape—not exactly conducive to perfect comfort, especially if two were trying to rest at the same time.

This predicament led to many curious inventions that brought us all the way to the luxurious springs and mattresses of the present. Ironically, there is now some agitation to get us back, for health reasons, to the hard wood-slatted bed of our forefathers by inserting a panel board under the mattress and over the spring.

Field beds, or canopy beds, with an arched and vaulted canopy, were so named because of their resemblance to tents pitched in a field. They, and canopy beds of all types, are far and away one of the most attractive of the utilitarian furnishings of colonial times. It is also interesting that their basic appearance has changed so very little since the time they were immediately equated with well-to-do Southern Colonial gentry. There were also high-poster beds both in New England

Queen Anne walnut chest of drawers and wardrobe with brass fittings. 1750.

Above and right. *Stamped brass escutcheon and teardrop drawer pull.*

Left. *Painted pine blanket chest. Hinged top opens to a deep well with two mock drawers over one working drawer. Painted in rose pink and oyster white. Massachusetts. 1731.*

Carved rosewood side chair and sofa made by John Henry Belter of New York in the mid 1800's.

and in Pennsylvania, their turnings made in the solid tradition of their particular locale. Rock maple posts weighing up to fifty pounds apiece and head and foot-boards of pine are still to be found in central New England. Heavy beech and butternut wood high-posters are also yet to be found in Berks and Lancaster counties in Pennsylvania. These posts with turnings of one piece were made from timbers over six inches square and seven feet long. The turnings were often carved in a modified tulip design and were polychromed in the reds, browns, blacks, and yellows of

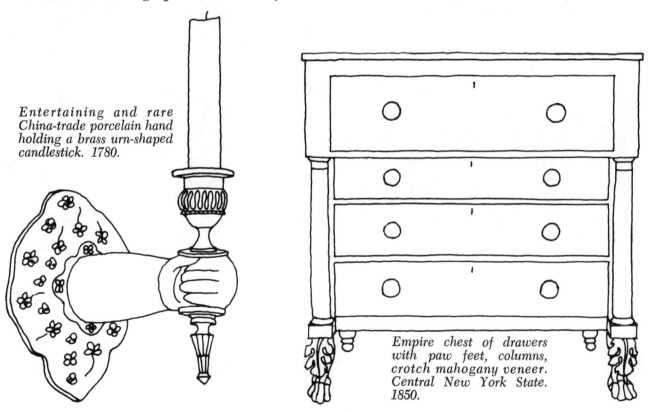

Entertaining and rare China-trade porcelain hand holding a brass urn-shaped candlestick. 1780.

Empire chest of drawers with paw feet, columns, crotch mahogany veneer. Central New York State. 1850.

the early Pennsylvania Dutch decor. Paneled head-boards and foot-boards were often striped and feather painted, paneled and scrolled.

Beds covering the 250 years from primitive colonial times to the late Victorian era are not difficult to identify with the period of their popularity. The earliest (primitive) and the latest (late Victorian) are again enjoying an impressive popularity. Perhaps it is because their simplicity and functional design allow them to harmonize even with the most modern decor. It also may be because it is now fashionable to be different and some of the ornate pieces of the late Victorian period compliment this trend. We might add that many of these old beds are still available and not yet too costly.

Although books covering the subject

Above. *Chippendale brass. This was a common and popular design. 1750–1775.*

Above. *Brass escutcheon of a common design. Keyhole was not always complemented with a lock.*

Early maple chest of drawers, typical of central New England. Graduated depth of drawers made it possible to use the same log for all wood facings.

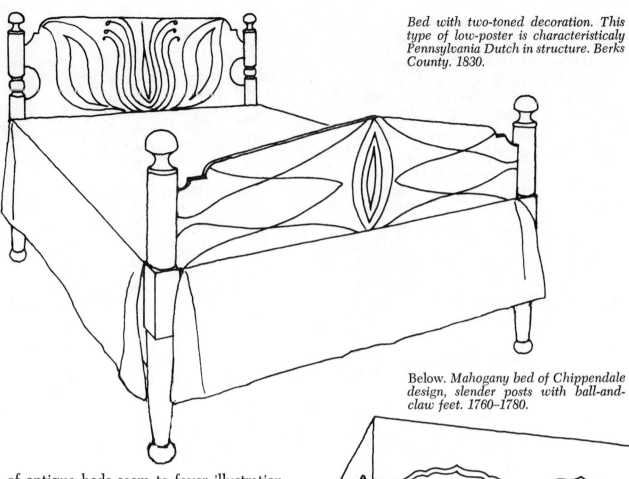

Bed with two-toned decoration. This type of low-poster is characteristicaly Pennsylvania Dutch in structure. Berks County. 1830.

Below. Mahogany bed of Chippendale design, slender posts with ball-and-claw feet. 1760–1780.

of antique beds seem to favor illustration of the field-type bed, the majority of beds were constructed with low posts. Early New England houses generally had ceilings not much over seven feet high and could not accommodate the high-posters so acceptable to city dwellers and landed gentry. Canopy beds were designed and made by some of the greatest cabinetmakers in Philadelphia, New York, and Boston. They have slender, tapered posts, fine turnings of rare woods, carvings, and high arched canopies covered with the finest brocades and lace, and are now treasured and still used by a surprising number of people.

We could not cover the subject of beds without mentioning several others, including the attractive and popular sleigh bed of the early nineteenth century. The Jenny Lind bed, designed by and named after the popular soprano, was a spool bed

Chest of drawers, decorated with a conventional design of 1825. Note that the design differs with the depth of each drawer. (Philadelphia Museum of Art)

Blown three-mold sparking lamp. Sparking lamps like this one were blown in molds used for making stoppers for quart decanters. Sandwich. 1825.

Below. *New England maple chest-on-chest, stamped-brass fittings, graduated drawers. 1750.*

with both the head and foot identical in size. It was probably the first couch or studio bed as we know them. Pine trees or pine cone turnings were popular motifs on New England low-post beds, as was the simple large ball turn at the top of maple low-posters.

At the same time, low-posters with adaptations of the ever-popular tulip motif were being made in all types of wood in the cabinet shops of Pennsylvania. Feather-painted and decorated or finished in natural grain, these sturdy low-post beds are still available in the Pennsylvania Dutch country.

As new materials became available, many kinds of beds followed these solid wood constructions. Iron and brass beds, with combinations of onyx and ormolu, were made by all sorts of metal workers. The market for these beds was extensive because the flat or banded spring was replacing the old rope and wood slats.

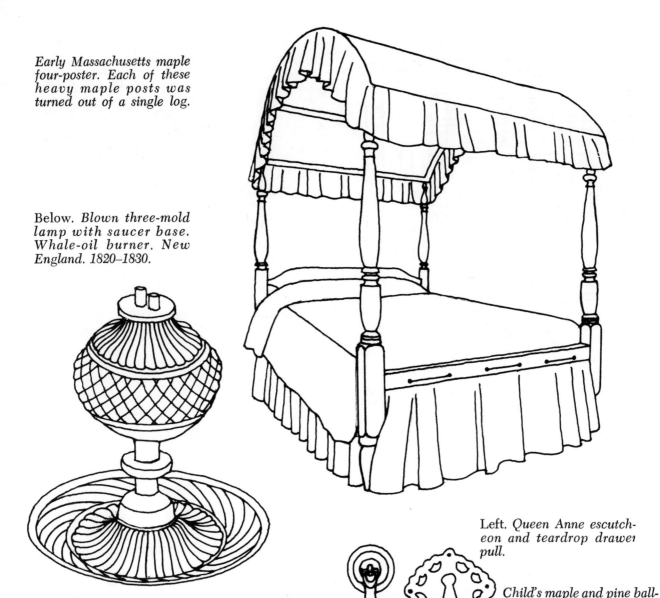

Early Massachusetts maple four-poster. Each of these heavy maple posts was turned out of a single log.

Below. *Blown three-mold lamp with saucer base. Whale-oil burner. New England. 1820–1830.*

Left. *Queen Anne escutcheon and teardrop drawer pull.*

Child's maple and pine ball-foot chest of drawers has three drawers with brass teardrop pulls.

It is little wonder that each of these styles of beds, so identifiable with its particular time, is a decorator's dream—for the choice is still great and the price accessible. All that is needed is taste and judgment and a little daring.

Antiques writers and critics of the last century played as important a role as the collectors, for then, as now, people who had the means and inclination to surround themselves with antiques did not necessarily have the taste or judgment to choose those items that would be of lasting value. And so, they leaned heavily upon the experts, self-styled or real. Although we may now find the artistic arrogance of many of these chroniclers absurd, we must

Below. *Openwork brass Chippendale drawer pull in a common design. 1760.*

Below. *Sparking lamp, just three inches high, blown from clear lead glass, one tube tin burner set in cork. New England. 1820.*

Chippendale carved mahogany chest of drawers, top with chamfered corners. Scrolled ogee bracket feet. Pennsylvania. Eighteenth century.

remember that they were often important and influential trend setters. The fact that they did not foresee the almost unbelievable future of this country is excusable, but the absolute didacticism of their artis-

tic intolerance occasionally becomes almost unbearable.

We cannot resist quoting another paragraph in which an author of those times takes a position on antiques which we are sure he felt to be helpful and carefully considered. It is one, though, that would have eliminated a large portion of today's amateur and interested collectors of mod-

"Six board" chest. The front and back boards are set into the "bootjack" ends, which were gracefully scrolled or cut with a simple "V". New England.

Stretcher table with octagonal top is an unusual variation of the more common square, round, or oval. Top is pine, base maple, painted barn red. Eighteenth century.

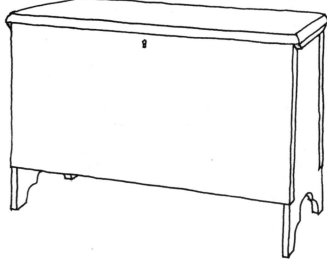

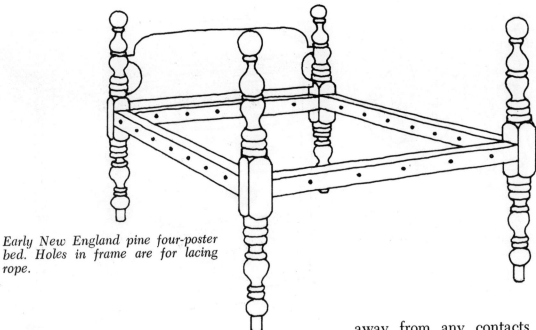

Early New England pine four-poster bed. Holes in frame are for lacing rope.

erate means for the very lack of antiques to collect. The quote is as follows:

By no possible stretch of the imagination could the hooked rug be called an artistic production. Its habitat is limited to a very small section of the country and it was never heard of until a few years ago when the junk of ancient farmhouse attics was tumbled out into the open daylight. To my way of thinking, the hooked rug is the horribly pathetic attempt of a feeble flame of artistic yearning in the mind of the farmer's wife or daughter, far, far away from any contacts with the world.

In a museum exhibiting the industries of the country or in a room reproducing a New England primitive homestead, hooked rugs should be included, but they are out of place in a home or *clubhouse* of elegance. Why should we be led astray by such crude productions as Sandwich glass, hooked rugs, Currier and Ives lithographs and plain pine furniture which totally misrepresented our country's past and present taste.

Left. The motifs used in woven coverlets—hearts, tulips, large and small stars—are most familiar. Below. Rose of Sharon around a starburst.

156

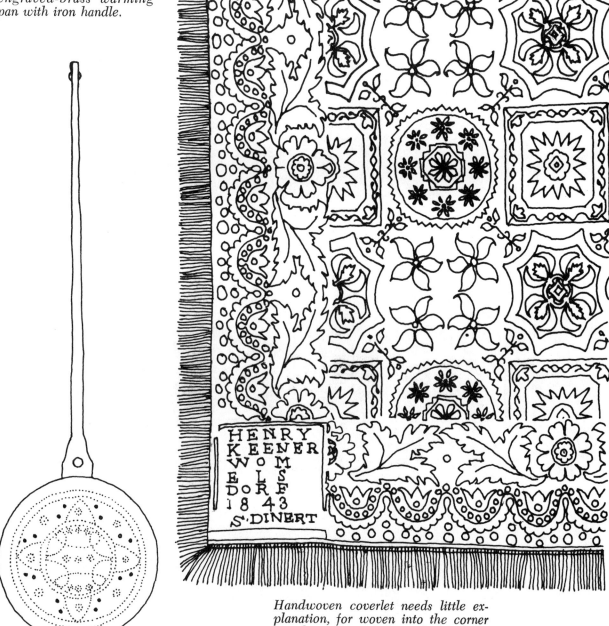

Below. *Eighteenth-century engraved-brass warming pan with iron handle.*

HENRY
KEENER
W O   M
E   L   S
D O R S F
1 8 4 3
S. DINERT

Handwoven coverlet needs little explanation, for woven into the corner are the names of the maker and the buyer, and the date.

Conversely, an equally eminent author of many books on antiques, Thomas H. Ormsbee, the grandson of Bradbury M. Barley, of Rutland, Vermont, the last of a well-known line of New England silversmiths, said on the subject, "Why even one good Currier and Ives, framed and hung on the wall, can make a room."

Incidentally, Mr. Ormsbee's generous

attitude concerning "good" antiques and the pleasures that can be derived from them is identical with our views on the subject.

The dominant note in the critical quote is its lack of feeling for people and change and the intrinsic beauty in artistic expression. Had we not sufficient reasons for writing this book, those negative paragraphs

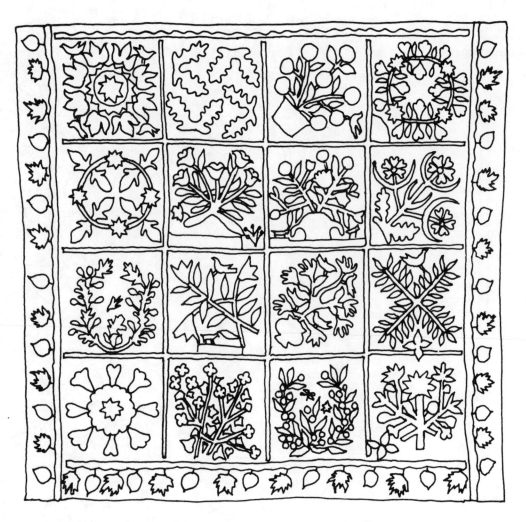

would have been sufficient motivation. For us, objects that do not reflect the spirit of the people are just things.

Were we to write on a subject that has been a most important influence in our lives, it would be on the subject of color.

It is not necessary to be an artist to have a feeling for color. Color is one of the earliest motivating influences in all our lives. Indeed, it has been demonstrated to be an established and obvious part of primitive life.

Six blocks from a quilt of forty-two different patches are shown on these two pages.

The appliqué quilt from York, Pennsylvania, on the opposite page is made of red, yellow, green, and blue bits of calico. The sixteen blocks are fitted together with bands of color. 1850.

The flowers and fruit as well as all the figures in these six appliqué patches are stylized. They are all the work of the same person.

It has often been said that the farmer painted his barns red because it was bright and was probably the cheapest weather preservative he could apply to its surface. Iron oxide mixed with linseed oil, a by-product of flax, was all he really needed, but the added bright color looked marvelous against the light and dark greens of the surrounding landscape in the summer and the white snow in the winter.

In New England, the shingles or shakes were not painted; they were left to weather to a dark brown or silvery gray de-

Artistic self-expression is evident in all appliqué. In some cases the bands of color indicate a regional preference.

"Six-board" pine blanket chest with a drawer. Pulls are New England type.

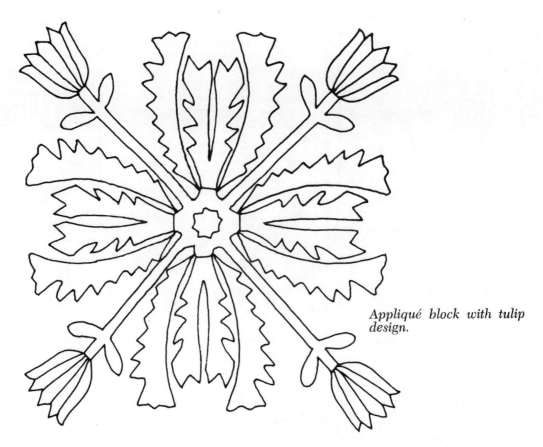

Appliqué block with tulip design.

pending on the wood they were made of. Color, as a protection against the elements, was applied to the roof surfaces and to the molding areas made of planking that were decorative details of the construction.

It is not surprising that although the touches of color in New England houses were confined to small and precious things within the house, the interiors in the more flamboyantly bright Pennsylvania Dutch country south of them were a riot of color.

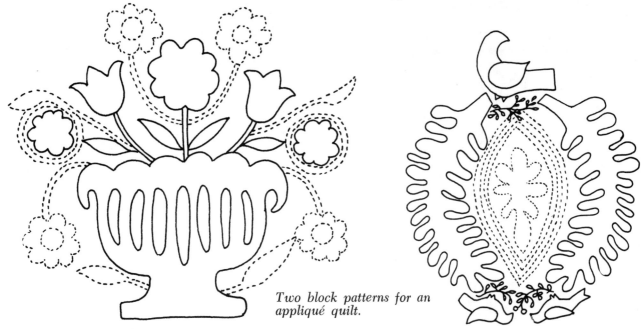

Two block patterns for an appliqué quilt.

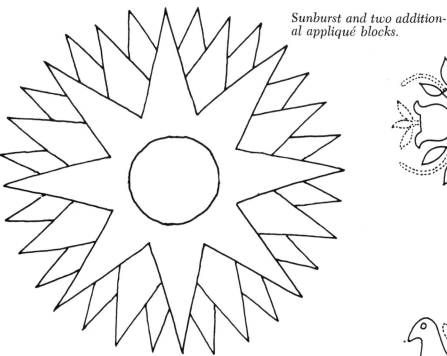

Sunburst and two additional appliqué blocks.

The Dutch people had little resistance to color, and a bucket of paint, whether white, red, blue, orange, or yellow, was like a cool drink before a thirsting man. It is typical that their gay and unreserved use of primary color was an instinctive part of their daily life, and it appeared in generous amounts wherever it could be applied.

To the colonial housewife, wastefulness was akin to sinfulness. This credo applied to every area of her life. When one thinks

The motifs selected for these two pages show the Pennsylvania Dutch woman to be an excellent designer. The primitive arrangements have balance, color, and infinite variety.

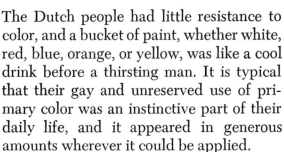

ELIS ABETH BUZIN

Pennsylvania dower chest shows Bavarian influence. The two drawers at base have brass pulls that appear to follow the same design as brasses made by Chippendale.

Shaving mugs, in popular demand as early as the 1860's, were imported without decoration from Bavaria or Limoges and, after 1890, from Germany, and were decorated in shops primarily in New York City to the specification of the buyer. Many carried the owner's name and a gaily painted symbol of his occupation.

about the prodigious labor it took to complete even a single household item at that time, it is astonishing that so much was done. If a dress was needed, yarn had to be made, woven, dyed, and fashioned into cloth before cutting and sewing could even be thought of.

It is no wonder that pieces of bright cotton brought across the ocean from English mills were carefully preserved. Remnants were cut into squares as small as an inch or two and were sewn together in the patterns we see in some of the early patchwork quilts. Like so many of the items made in those times, the quilts were both artistic and utilitarian. Although many of these quilts are highly prized by collectors, it is extremely difficult for the inexperienced to gauge the age of a quilt. It is almost necessary to be an expert on fabrics, for the same designs and

Above. *Simple flower motif hooked rug.* Below. *New England hooked rug made about 1830, worked in shades of beige and brown.* (Shelburne Museum, Shelburne, Vermont)

stitches are still used in the same painstaking way by country people today. The market for this product is ever-increasing, and we might add, so is the price.

In everyone's past there was a favorite toy that has since become the symbol of a time, a place, or an unforgettable recollection from one's childhood. For a woman, nothing will obliterate the memory of the favorite doll of her earliest years. Prior to the middle 1700's, most references to dolls referred to puppets, for dolls of that time were made to represent adults, not babies or children as we know dolls today. Through the centuries, dolls have been made of rags, china, wood, plaster or equally perishable bisque, celluloid, rubber, wax, papier-maché, and presently in the ever-increasing types of plastic.

The earliest dolls known to have existed in our colonial times were made of straw or cornhusks. Their crudely shaped heads carved of wood were the artistic result of an affectionate father's creative efforts to please his young daughter. The vivid imagination of the child took care of all the rest.

The history of this interesting and emo-

Four-poster in the Chippendale style with turned posts and straight square legs ending in block feet.

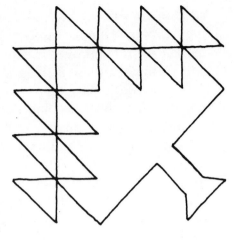

Patchwork quilt designs: Left, "Missouri Star." Right, "Pine Tree," a colonial favorite. Below. "Mountain Pink," a delicate pattern.

Below. The intricate "Lucinda's Star."

tional subject has filled many books but there is very little that touches on the subject of American-made dolls in those early times. The European doll was masterfully made and was of great interest to the colonist, for the dolls' dresses brought important fashion news from the capitals of Europe. As such, they were a popular item for women as well as for children to collect.

As objects of decoration, dolls hold a place similar to paintings: Both are representative of the people of the time and the place of their origin. Although there

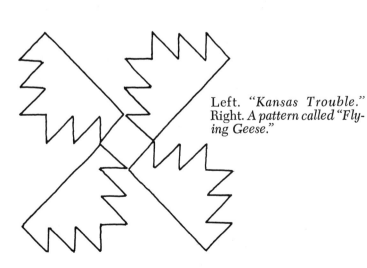

Left. "Kansas Trouble." Right. A pattern called "Flying Geese."

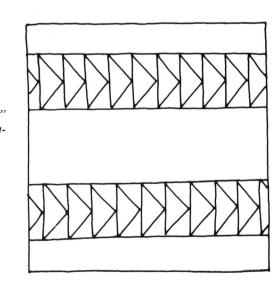

164

The triple sunflower quilt pattern is a combination of pieced and appliquéd work: The flowers are pieced and the stems and leaves appliquéd. Each block of three sunflowers and one stem is twelve inches square.

Below. Sheraton high-poster field bed, ogee canopy frame. 1790–1800.

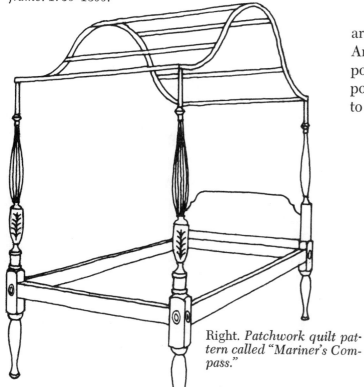

are very few existing examples of Colonial American dolls, we do know from contemporary writings that a doll was just as important to the child of those times as it is to today's child. As such, dolls certainly de-

Right. Patchwork quilt pattern called "Mariner's Compass."

Trundle bed with buttons for lacing rope. These low beds were pushed under the higher beds during the day.

Left. Bow-back side chair with plank seat was made for a child. 1770.

Toy cradle, only twelve inches long, of pine. Central New England primitive.

Below. Charming Windsor love seat made for a child. Pennsylvania. 1760.

serve their proper place in any book on American antiques. Dollmaking was an art and because dolls were not manufactured in this country until the middle of the 1800's, the few on record were made individually with loving care and certainly deserve our attention.

All through the nineteenth century the references to dolls usually meant those that were imported from France and Germany. After the late 1800's, increased interest in the subject brought about the

Right. Child's pine rocking horse. New England primitive.

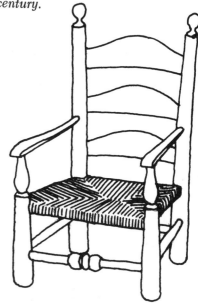

Left. *Quilt made of diamond-shaped patches in a star design was intended for a child's bed.*

Right. *Child's slat-back chair with reed seat, Chippendale-style stretcher and ball finials. Early eighteenth century.*

making of dolls of American design and manufacture. The first American-made dolls closely followed the European style, that is, the dolls were adults and their function was to represent new fashions or other current newsworthy subjects.

Dolls made in the image of popular personalities of the stage captured the public's imagination and were particularly in demand in Victorian times. The Waterbury Watch Company, possibly influenced by animated dolls imported from Germany, became interested in this vogue and its potential and turned their clock-making know-how to the seemingly lucra-

tive field. They are reputed to have animated some of the very few American-made walking dolls.

Most of the fine collections of dolls in this country are made up of a predominance of European imports with only an occasional doll of native American origin.

It was not until the turn of the twentieth century that dolls, as we know them,

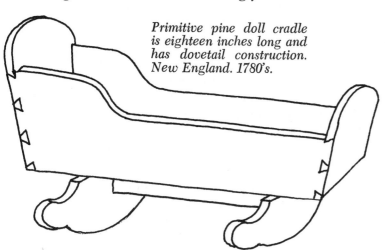

Primitive pine doll cradle is eighteen inches long and has dovetail construction. New England. 1780's.

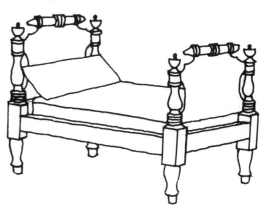

Miniature bed made for child's toy has carved horizontal bars across the headboard and footboard. On top of the posts are urns. 1820.

Handsome "Whig Rose" appliqué quilt with an interesting scalloped border.

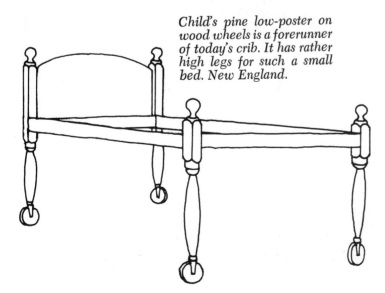

Child's pine low-poster on wood wheels is a forerunner of today's crib. It has rather high legs for such a small bed. New England.

became a widely popular American item; now, some sixty or seventy years later, they have become an important feature in American collections. Although dolls from the early colonial times are exceedingly rare, there are dolls similar in construction to English wax dolls of the 1820's to be found in well-known collections in Vermont and Massachusetts. But, despite the dolls' similarity of construction, little is actually known of their origin.

Although the dolls of early periods are hard to find, there is much available classified as doll furniture. Wherever possible, we have recorded pieces in our illustrations. But we must caution you that

Above. *Appliqué design for "Tulip" crib quilt.*

Right. *"Rose of Sharon" appliqué quilt.*

Left. *The Boston rocker with the familiar roll seat and arms—the most popular chair ever made.*

some of the larger pieces of doll furniture might actually have been made for a small child. There is no way to be absolutely sure.

It is entertaining to study the dolls made prior to 1900: their proportions are those of an adult and they are dressed in the popular adult fashions of their time.

It was not until the early twentieth century that dolls took on the baby conformation so familiar to us now. It is amusing to note that with the increasing popularity and enormous interest in dolls, a great many dolls are now made to look like toddlers and even teenagers. Perhaps they will return to their original and adult form of centuries ago.

Floor cloths, the early American forerunner of carpeting, were widely used, as were broad patterns and stencil designs painted to add color underfoot. Freehand designs or geometric patterns stenciled in the style of floor tiles as early as 1720

remain to be seen. Spatter painting on floors has also suffered much from wear: The paint itself had too little varnish and gloss to withstand rough daily usage over a long period of time. There are still, however, a few fine examples of this

Right. *New England maple and pine cradle of unusual design. The maple posts are 2¾ inches square.*

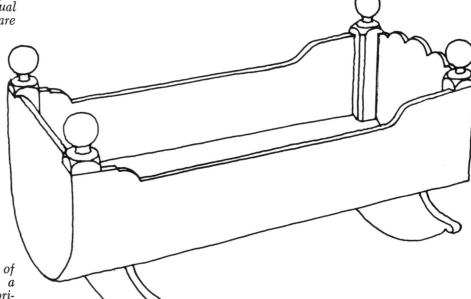

Opposite page. *"Tree of Life" crib quilt shows a basic motif of ancient origin. In this Pennsylvania-Dutch application, birds, berries, oak and ivy leaves are used. The leaves are correctly veined in tiny quilting stitches. 1875.*

Below. *Diminutive Pennsylvania chest, eight inches high, seventeen inches long, is beautifully decorated in red, blue, black, and green on a background of antique white.*

quaint art yet to be seen in Barnstable on Cape Code. Spatter, one of the later floor-decorating techniques, became popular after the mid-nineteenth century. However, it was so well reproduced much later that the original examples of this primitive art form are difficult to distinguish.

THE DEN

A careful study of interior painting, stenciling, decorating, and fractur can be valuable because it is basic to coordinating the furnishings in a room. This is true whether you wish the room to reflect the period of its furnishings or you would rather place your antiques in a more eclec-tic setting. The choice of decorating styles is unlimited; rooms can be beautifully done in the highly decorative mood of the late Victorian era, in the simple, colorful primitive Pennsylvania Dutch style, or in the prime and polished New England fash-ion. Again, you might choose the open

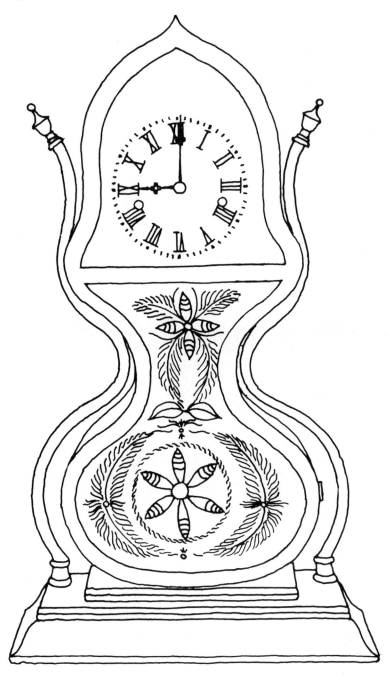

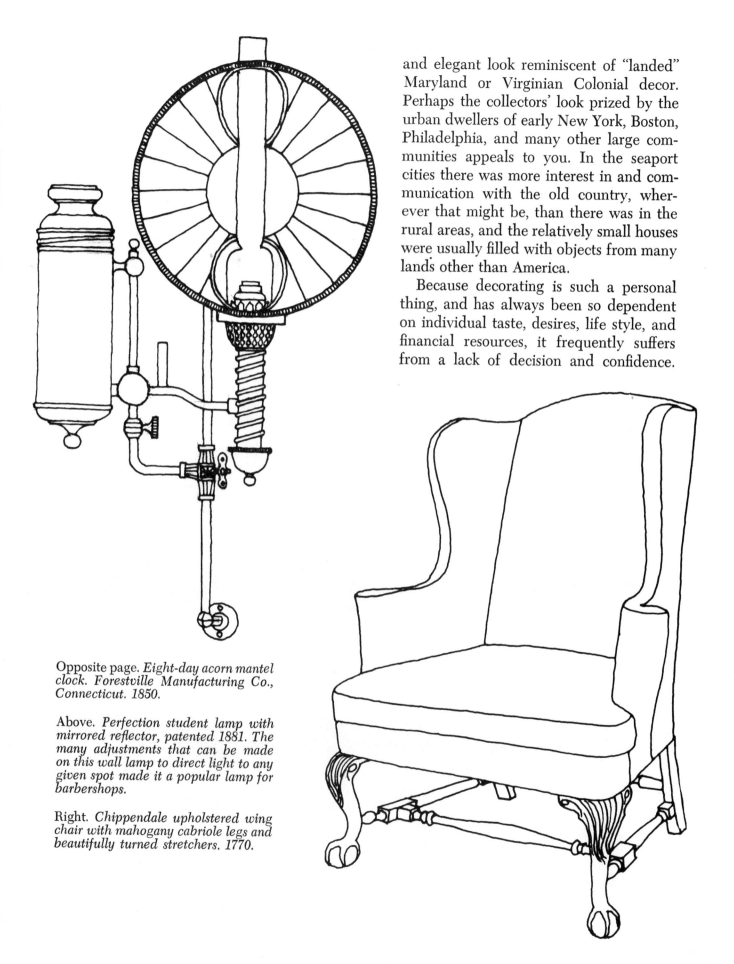

and elegant look reminiscent of "landed" Maryland or Virginian Colonial decor. Perhaps the collectors' look prized by the urban dwellers of early New York, Boston, Philadelphia, and many other large communities appeals to you. In the seaport cities there was more interest in and communication with the old country, wherever that might be, than there was in the rural areas, and the relatively small houses were usually filled with objects from many lands other than America.

Because decorating is such a personal thing, and has always been so dependent on individual taste, desires, life style, and financial resources, it frequently suffers from a lack of decision and confidence.

Opposite page. *Eight-day acorn mantel clock. Forestville Manufacturing Co., Connecticut. 1850.*

Above. *Perfection student lamp with mirrored reflector, patented 1881. The many adjustments that can be made on this wall lamp to direct light to any given spot made it a popular lamp for barbershops.*

Right. *Chippendale upholstered wing chair with mahogany cabriole legs and beautifully turned stretchers. 1770.*

173

Left. *Polychromed rooster carved of pine, found in New York State.* (Museum of Modern Art)

Above. *Cast-iron rabbit, painted white, was probably used as an ornament on the lawn or the hearth.*

This is particularly true today, when one is constantly confronted with ideas on every subject pertaining to decor in every medium of communication. Expressing one's individual artistic and decorating opinions seems much more difficult now than it would have been in colonial days. Of course, people imitated one another then, just as they do now, but because of the geographical isolation of many of the homes in this big country, there were a number of very individual decorating

Bennington reclining doe flower-holder is dated 1849.

bove. The Franklin stove in this room is as practical ~ it is attractive. With the cover removed from its ~ont it can be used as the iron fireplace it was designed ~ be. Early 1800's.

Above. *The Pennsylvania dry sink serves perfectly as a bar in the den, with its breadboard top open or closed. The balloon-back chair is both colorful and comfortable. Pressed-glass decanters are Victorian, as is the bracket lamp. Water pitcher is salt glaze.*

Left. *Large American pewter plates eighteen inches or more in diameter are hard to come by. Their very size and weight caused many to be destroyed while still in use. The candlestick is Vaseline glass and quite early, as is the kerosene lamp of flint glass blown into a mold. The taller decorated lamp is Victorian.*

Above. A late Victorian medallion-back sofa and a very early spinning wheel are seen in the hall of this stone house built in the 1770's. On the second level is a New England slat-back chair with a rush seat and a late ogee clock.

Left. The upstairs hall has a very early bench-table of pine. The chest with the ogee feet is feather-painted, and the braided rug is a fine example of New England work around 1840.

Below. An extremely early pine sea chest and a skein counter are part of this front hall. The door, and its latch and hinges, is original.

Above. *Pennsylvania Windsor writing armchair with drawer under seat. 1770.*

Left. *This very popular type of lamp was made of both tin and stamped brass. 1860.*

Above. *Early pine corner cabinet with single panel door in base, "H" hinges of wrought iron. Central New England.*

Below. *Primitive stretcher table with splayed legs. Pennsylvania. Eighteenth century.*

innovations. The results were dictated in great part by the ethnic background and exposure of the person who was planning to decorate. As such, the finished products of these personal artistic expressions reflect not only the personality of the individuals who lived in the house, but tell us a great deal about how they lived.

Naturally, the decorating styles of the past were developed to complement the furnishings available in their own times. As such, they are valuable references for those who wish to duplicate period rooms in their entirety. This, of course, is the objective of many museum collections. And for museums, it is quite correct to record and not to invent. We feel, however, that a little of this goes a long way and though we enjoy living with antiques, we must live with them on our own terms. They must not be allowed to get in the way of our twentieth-century living.

In our research in the broad subject of decorating, we have found many dubious experts. We would like to quote one statement in particular, concerning paintings: "Imitating primitive painting is quite easy." As artists, we can only suggest that this is a rather uninformed statement, for primitive painting is a most difficult form of artistic expression to imitate: When one has enough technical know-how to attempt it, this very craftmanship will undoubtedly get in the way of a successful primitive result. We use this example to point out that slavish imitation in decorating of any type rarely works. Be original! In so doing, the warmth of originality will not suffer from imitation, nor will your home lose a bit of its charm because it is not a duplication of someone else's. Imitation in dec-

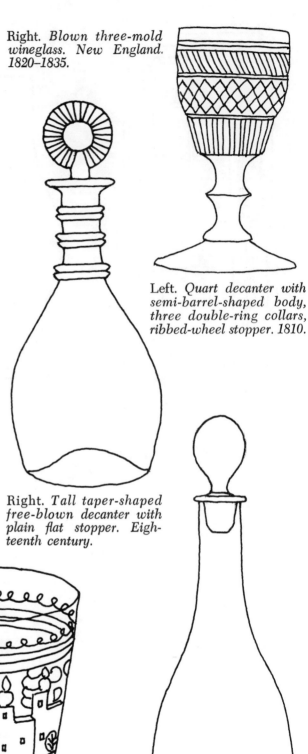

Right. *Blown three-mold wineglass. New England. 1820–1835.*

Left. *Quart decanter with semi-barrel-shaped body, three double-ring collars, ribbed-wheel stopper. 1810.*

Left. *Blown three-piece-mold quart decanter and stopper. Arch and fern leaf pattern with medallion.*

Right. *Tall taper-shaped free-blown decanter with plain flat stopper. Eighteenth century.*

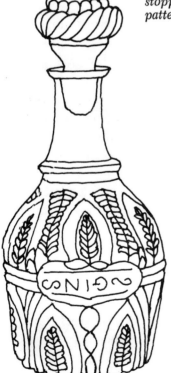

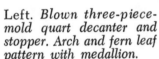

Above. *Drinking glass with steeple-design polychrome enamel decoration.*

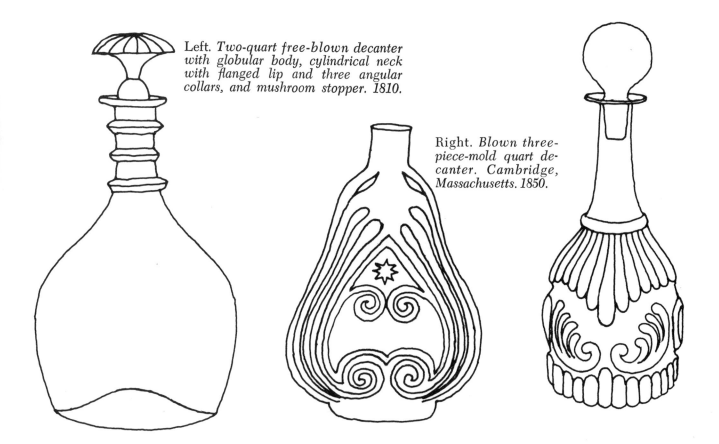

Left. *Two-quart free-blown decanter with globular body, cylindrical neck with flanged lip and three angular collars, and mushroom stopper. 1810.*

Right. *Blown three-piece-mold quart decanter. Cambridge, Massachusetts. 1850.*

orating produces much the same artistic loss that a handmade article suffers when manufactured in quantity—no matter how well it is duplicated, it is not original.

High on the list of originators in the early colonial days was Rufus Porter, who began his most artistic and most inventive career in the early 1800's. Born on a farm in Boxford, Massachusetts, he set out to decorate whatever he could find where-ever there was interest in his artistry. A sort of Johnny Appleseed of art, he painted houses, signs, portraits, and decorated interior walls of houses. Like many

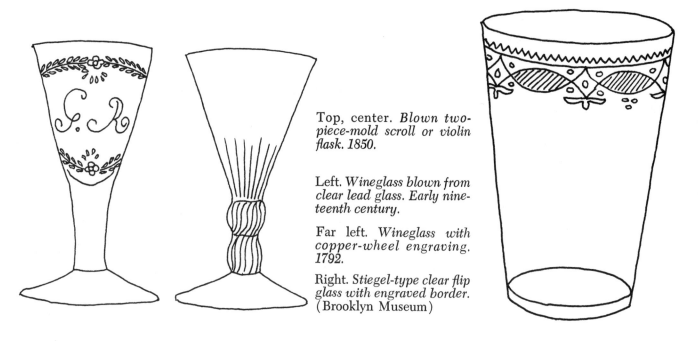

Top, center. *Blown two-piece-mold scroll or violin flask. 1850.*

Left. *Wineglass blown from clear lead glass. Early nineteenth century.*

Far left. *Wineglass with copper-wheel engraving. 1792.*

Right. *Stiegel-type clear flip glass with engraved border.* (Brooklyn Museum)

artists before and after him, his interests ran a wide gamut: He was a teacher, inventor, musician, and dancing master, and his writing brought him into the publishing field where he is said to have founded and performed as editor of *The New York Mechanic* and the still-published and respected *Scientific American*. His book, *The Curious Arts*, published in 1825 when he was about thirty-three years old, which included a treatise on landscape painting, was widely circulated, for by that time Porter had many admirers and followers, and had decorated almost a hundred homes throughout the New England area. About fifteen years later, he published some of the first "how to" articles on the subject of landscape painting on walls. These were all part of a continuing series of articles covering portrait painting, painting on glass, carriage

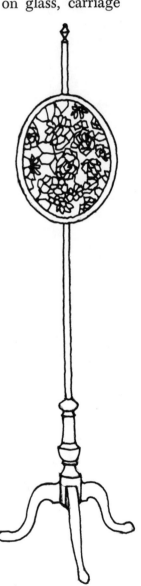

Above. *Mahogany fire screen. Newport. 1780–1790.*

Left. *Fire screen. Massachusetts. 1765–1780.*

Right. *Fire screen with needlepoint floral design.*

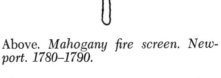

ornamentation and striping, window shades, and walls.

Although Porter thought of himself as a decorator rather than a painter, his orginal and unaffected painting is a true presentation of American folk art, or primitive painting as we know it today.

There were many itinerant artists at the same time. Joseph Leavitt, in particular, left his important and colorful mark all over New England.

Left. Fire screen made of scrolled walnut has an unusual utility shelf. Pennsylvania. 1740–1750.

Above. Painted wood and leather fireplace bellows. Vermont. Early 1800's.

Left. Mahogany fire-screen with needlepoint. Newport. 1750–1760.

Wallpapers imported from France and England were available only as luxuries but the itinerant painter was able to bring to the rural communities the touch of color and design that wallpapers made available to the well-to-do urban person. Patterned, stenciled, and landscaped walls began to appear as far west as Ohio and Kentucky, as New Englanders settled in those areas and brought with them the ever-present need for color and decoration. Stencils were more usual than free-hand painting, for it was possible to do this kind of design duplication without artistic training. The colors used were usually earthy and primary—oxides and coarse ground pigments mixed into a base of skimmed milk, referred to as "buttermilk paint."

In Pennsylvania, where most house construction was of stone, little area remained for the use of paint and decoration. However, the Swiss barns, so charac-

Above. *Stanley's #1 chunk-wood stove. The extra casting in the stovepipe functioned as a radiator.*

Below and right. *The Franklin stove, invented in 1742 by Benjamin Franklin, saved much wood, produced more heat, and rid small rooms of smoke. It was designed of standardized parts that could be assembled in most fireplaces.*

Right. *Elegant wood-burning stove made in 1857. The cast-iron vase on top was for water and acted as a room humidifier.*

182

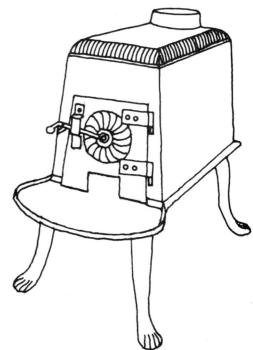

Left. *The Arcand parlor stove had interchangeable drafts and loading doors to permit use in almost any part of the room.*

Right. *Primitive front-loading box-type heater. Large door is for chunk wood and has an opening for a constant base draft.*

be seen, the geometric patterns of the hex signs are most familiar to visitors in Pennsylvania. Broad white lines indicating arched doors and windows were drawn on the red painted wood and are said to

Right. *Decorative cast-iron stoves like this were made in foundries in Albany, Buffalo, Baltimore, Pittsburgh, Boston, New York, and New Orleans from 1848 until 1878.*

teristic a part of rural Pennsylvania, made up for this. These barns were usually built on a steep slope, much the same as their Swiss counterparts. Stone was used for the down-slope, stall area, and the side walls. The up-slope area, in which the hay and feed were stored, was constructed of wood and became a natural area for decoration. Although there are many freehand murals of barnyard subject matter still to

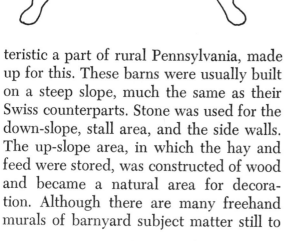

have been painted to extend those door and window areas visually to confuse witches attempting to fly into the barn. Most authorities on the subject of hex signs agree that although these designs might have had a talismanic origin, decorating barns was really the visual expression of a need for color in the Pennsylvania Dutch.

Fractur painting is an adaptation of European manuscript illumination. The

Above. *Wrought-iron andirons with looped finials and spit hooks below.*

Above left. *Stove plate by Henry Wilhelm ("Baron") Stiegel, who operated the Elizabeth Furnace, named after his wife.* Below left. *A German box or jamb stove.*

Cast-iron, painted "Hessian Soldier" andiron, one of a pair. Late eighteenth century.

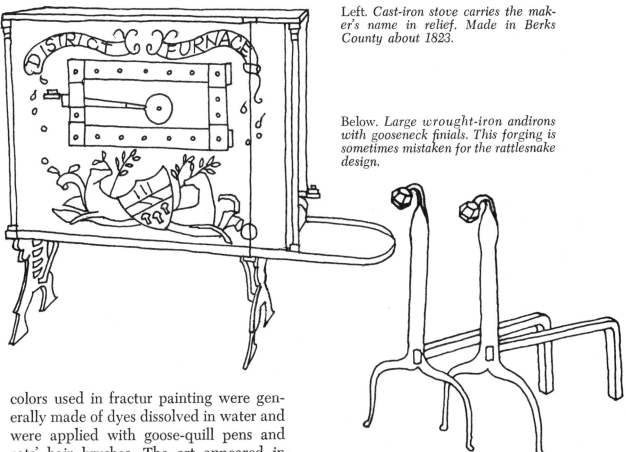

Left. *Cast-iron stove carries the maker's name in relief. Made in Berks County about 1823.*

Below. *Large wrought-iron andirons with gooseneck finials. This forging is sometimes mistaken for the rattlesnake design.*

colors used in fractur painting were generally made of dyes dissolved in water and were applied with goose-quill pens and cats' hair brushes. The art appeared in Pennsylvania as early as 1730 and continued to the end of the nineteenth century. Fractur is often seen on birth certificates and baptismal certificates and these attractive polychromed documents are much sought after for framing and decorating walls. The earliest fractur was usually religious in subject matter and was popular with many of the sects of Pennsylvania, including Dunkard, Mennonite, Amish, and Moravian.

Itinerant penmen traveled from one community to another and left their writing and illumination on certificates of birth, death, baptism, and marriage. They often decorated motto wall pieces and bookplates. Indeed, they decorated almost any object for which they could charge a fee.

Some of the better known craftsmen or fractur artists were Francis Portzeline, Martin Brechall, and Heinrich Otto,

Below. *Iron stove plate with typical tulip and heart motifs of the Pennsylvania Dutch.*

Right. *30-inch-high shelf clock, with quadrangular case, molded arch cornice, bracket feet, and white painted dial. Titus Merriman, Bristol, Connecticut. 1810. Below. Pairs of early brass clock hands.*

whose works can still be identified on personal items as well as dower chests found mainly in the Lancaster County area. Fractur wedding certificates are often found mounted inside the lids of these dower chests, both the certificate and the chest having been painted for the bride's family by the same artist.

Although most fractur was European in origin, it was practiced in the Colonies following the War of Independence. Soon it developed a typically American style—broader and bolder in pattern—and featured many symbols important in the New World. This new expression of an Old World art caused fractur to become a true American folk art. In fact, early nineteenth century examples are almost free of the earlier European influences.

Chippendale slant-front desk. New England. Eighteenth century.

Right. *Two early brass clock hands.* Far right. *"Marbleized" clock. Ingraham and Co. 1880.*

Below. *Shelf clock with kidney dial by Benjamin Morrel of New Hampshire. 1820.*

Currier and Ives were perhaps the most popular recorders of the American scene from 1840 to 1875. A charming review of Americans at home, at play, in their occupations, was recorded in the vivid and colorful lithographs that appeared two or three generations prior to the advent of illustrated magazines. The lithographs, printed from drawings on stone, left little in the way of subject matter concerning

Above. *Wood knob used in seventeenth and eighteenth centuries.* Right. *Schoolmaster's pine desk. About 1840.*

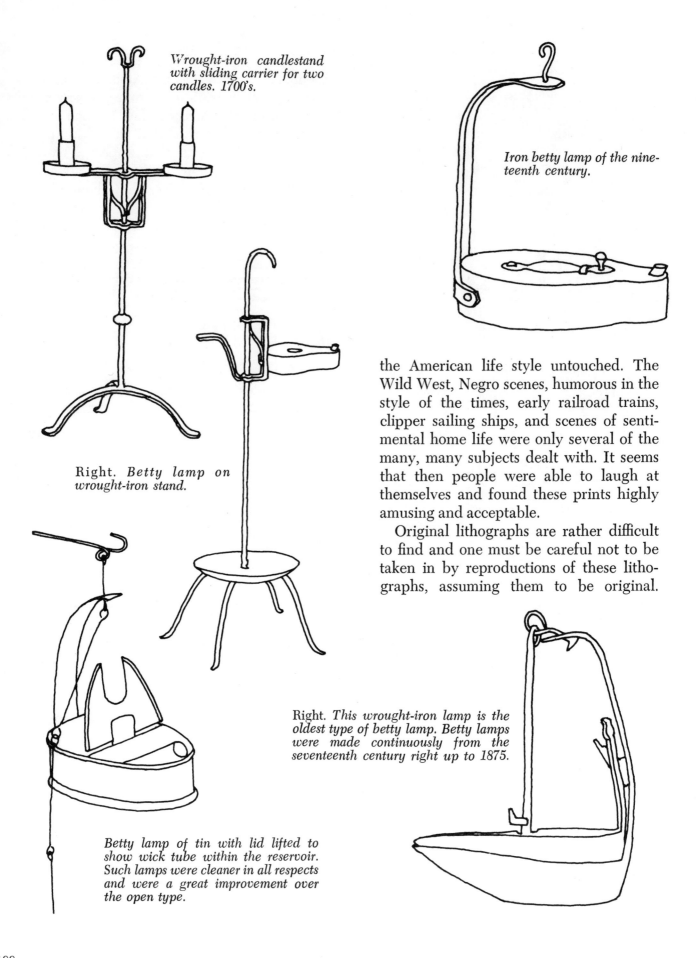

Wrought-iron candlestand with sliding carrier for two candles. 1700's.

Iron betty lamp of the nineteenth century.

Right. Betty lamp on wrought-iron stand.

the American life style untouched. The Wild West, Negro scenes, humorous in the style of the times, early railroad trains, clipper sailing ships, and scenes of sentimental home life were only several of the many, many subjects dealt with. It seems that then people were able to laugh at themselves and found these prints highly amusing and acceptable.

Original lithographs are rather difficult to find and one must be careful not to be taken in by reproductions of these lithographs, assuming them to be original.

Right. This wrought-iron lamp is the oldest type of betty lamp. Betty lamps were made continuously from the seventeenth century right up to 1875.

Betty lamp of tin with lid lifted to show wick tube within the reservoir. Such lamps were cleaner in all respects and were a great improvement over the open type.

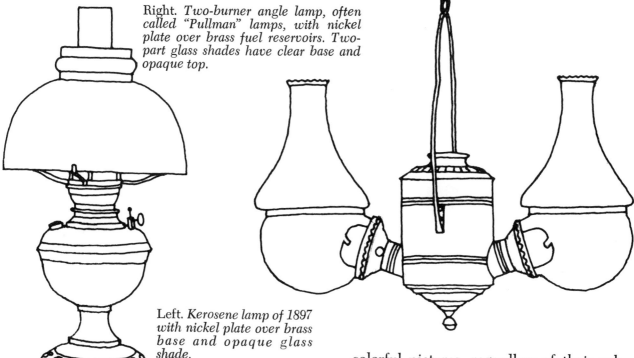

Right. *Two-burner angle lamp, often called "Pullman" lamps, with nickel plate over brass fuel reservoirs. Two-part glass shades have clear base and opaque top.*

Left. *Kerosene lamp of 1897 with nickel plate over brass base and opaque glass shade.*

There were, of course, many other prints made at the same time and in the same style, for up until that period there had been little available in the way of pictures for wall decoration and printers were busy filling that need. Paintings were mainly European and expensive; the American Primitive had not yet been discovered and American representational painting had not yet come into being. Those few artists who painted for the more wealthy classes confined their work to portraiture or, in some cases, murals, usually beautiful and fanciful landscapes that decorated rooms in elegant plantation homes. The more primitive painter confined his talents to livestock murals on the outside of barns, a fascinating decor that can still be seen on the barns in the Pennsylvania Dutch country in and around Virginsville. The sgraffito plates of the Dutch country and the woodcuts found on early baptismal records demonstrate that even then there was a strong desire to decorate, and to frame and hang colorful pictures, regardless of their subject matter, on the walls, just as there is now. It is rather surprising to discover that a great many of these pictures are still hung in homes for their artistic qualifications rather than for their amusing antiquity and association with earlier times.

Iron was discovered early in the eighteenth century in eastern Pennsylvania. This was a coarse quality of low-grade ore called "bog iron" and was usually found in surface veins. Furnaces were quickly set up near and around Philadelphia to

Angle lamp with brass fuel oil reservoir. 1875.

Above. *Bulldog bank. 1885.*

Right. *Pelican savings bank. A mocking cashier's face appears when the coin is deposited. In 1878 this mechanical bank sold for one dollar.*

Left. *Cast-iron mechanical toy bank, "Speaking Dog." Upon pressing a plunger, the lid of the seat opens to receive the coin placed in the girl's paddle. The coin drops as her arm rises. At the same time, the dog opens his mouth and wags his tail. Made in the Stevens Foundry, Cromwell, Connecticut. Patented 1885.*

smelt this ore as early as 1716. There are also records of a low-grade iron ore mined and poured into crude shot at furnaces located at the foot of the Berkshire Mountains of central Massachusetts. Years later, that iron shot was said to have been used by the Green Mountain Boys in the Revolutionary War. Although iron was often used as ballast in the holds of the sailing ships that came to the Colonies, nevertheless, only the smallest amount of it found its way into daily use. Because of its lack, New Englanders learned to pin the tim-

bers of their houses together with rock maple stakes and to "join" their woodworking with the strongest dovetails and mortise and tenons. The little iron they owned could be found in kitchens in the form of pots, cranes, and, with luck, a few knives. It was no secret, however, that iron made things last longer and run better and that as a commodity it definitely improved one's standard of living. The short supply of this basic metal in New England becomes more apparent if one studies the work of the blacksmiths of the

Above. *Frog bank. When the coin is deposited in the frog's mouth, he gulps it down and rolls his eyes.*

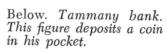

Below. *Tammany bank. This figure deposits a coin in his pocket.*

Above. *The Presto bank. When the coin is inserted a mouse pops out of the roof.*

early eighteenth century in that area. The method by which the local blacksmiths would draw the metal from the raw pig iron was an indication of the value they attached to it. They forged it in a way that allowed them to get the most they could out of every pennyweight of it;

strap hinges with thin curls or rattails were as delicate as possible, and cranes for the fireplaces were drawn out on the anvil to a thinness only just sufficient to support the cooking ware to be suspended from them. When contrasted with the heavy trammels, cooking chains, and the generous weight of the forgings made by the Pennsylvania ironmaker, it is easy to see

Below. *Mechanical bank patented by Mr. C. C. Johnson, of Windsor, Vermont. When a penny is placed on the tray, the cashier enters one door of the bank, deposits the coin inside, and comes out the other door.*

Trick pony bank. The coin is deposited in the pony's mouth. When the lever at back is pulled out, his neck bends down and the coin is dropped into the trough, the bottom of which opens to receive it.

Toy locomotive of painted tin and cast iron. The unwound spring shows between the rear wheels. Nineteenth century.

that the raw material was available in Pennsylvania but not in New England.

As a member of the community, the blacksmiths held a prestigious position in the early settlements. They were artists and craftsmen, responsible for the strong and enduring tools and utensils so essential to the bare necessities of colonial life: axes to clear the land for farming, farm tools to work the land, metalwork for the carts and wagons that transported the produce, hinges, nails, belts, knives, forks, cooking utensils. It was not until 1761 that the first cooking stove, its conception attributed to Thomas Maybury, was cast at Hereford Furnace in Pennsylvania. Although barely resembling the cookstoves that followed later, it was the first heating stove with a surface for cooking. It had no removable lids, but because of its flat top surface, it eliminated the necessity of the long-legged cooking utensils previously made to sit in the hot coals of the fire-

Cast-iron mechanical toy bank, "Teddy and the Bear," was made in the Stevens Foundry, Cromwell, Connecticut.

Steamboat bank, dated before 1900, is nonmechanical and was fashioned to resemble a Mississippi riverboat.

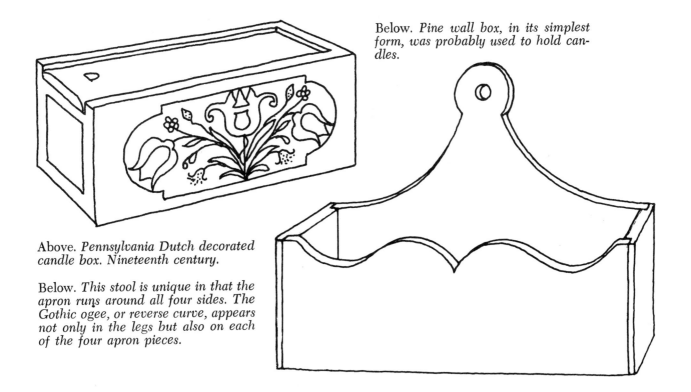

Above. *Pennsylvania Dutch decorated candle box. Nineteenth century.*

Below. *This stool is unique in that the apron runs around all four sides. The Gothic ogee, or reverse curve, appears not only in the legs but also on each of the four apron pieces.*

Below. *Pine wall box, in its simplest form, was probably used to hold candles.*

place. This gave the housewife the opportunity to polish the bottom of her pots, a dubious privilege but one in which she seemed to take great pride.

The blacksmiths, whose almost indestructible forgings and castings have immortalized their artistry and creativeness, proved again that once the essential utilitarian form of an object has been resolved, the creative need to decorate blossoms forth. Craftsmen usually expressed their artistic motivations in original designs or in representations of the nature about them. The men working in iron, true to this instinct, produced patterns, castings, and forgings of great beauty. It

is sad that due credit cannot be given to the unknown men who created the decorative molds from which the castings were made, but it is a consolation to know that their works will be forever admired.

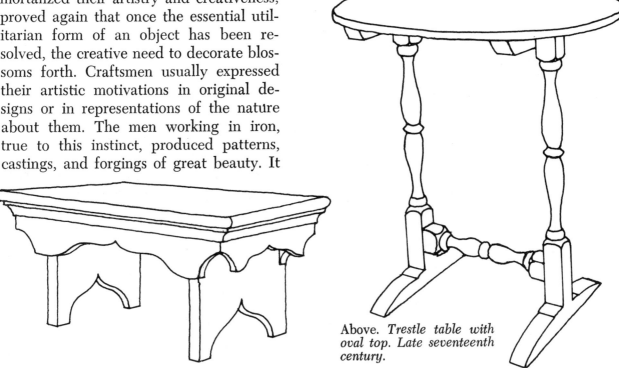

Above. *Trestle table with oval top. Late seventeenth century.*

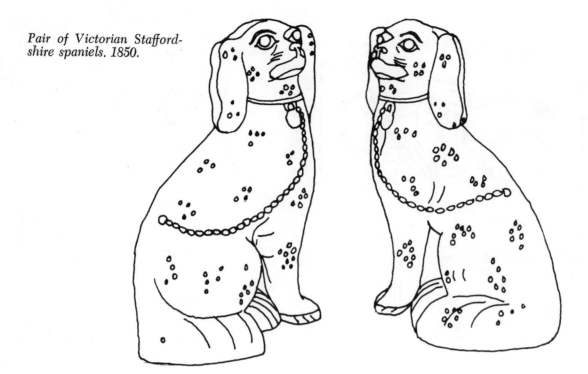

Pair of Victorian Stafford-shire spaniels. 1850.

About 1745, when Benjamin Franklin invented the Franklin stove, that famous half-stove, half-fireplace, he caused quite a stir. The fireplacelike draft of the open front of the Franklin stove consumed great quantities of fuel and at the same time created an excessive amount of heat, not necessarily agreeable to the English colonists with their normal resistance to being too warm. In a like fashion, the Germans preferred their decorative square iron stoves, because the slower burning

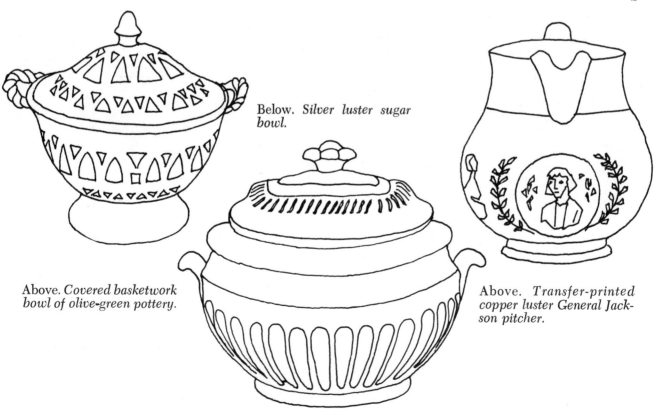

Below. *Silver luster sugar bowl.*

Above. *Covered basketwork bowl of olive-green pottery.*

Above. *Transfer-printed copper luster General Jackson pitcher.*

and economy of these traditional heating devices were familiar to them.

Forgings are representative of a time when living was simpler but when each activity called for a great expenditure of individual effort. If one wanted to have something done, it was best to get busy and do it oneself. Early iron forgings and castings still do not look out of place in a home today, although they are no longer essential to our daily needs. Iron is, of course, exceedingly heavy, and so, when used for decorating purposes, it is impractical to move it from place to place. It is usually most pleasing and appropriate when used as a fireplace ornament, for this is where it originally functioned and could still function if called upon to do so. We feel that this idea of getting maximum use out of every item in the house is essentially Colonial American in spirit.

When identifying early pieces of furniture, the small bits of iron that were used in their making are often a clue to the date of their manufacture. Rat-tail hinges

Above. *Small copper-luster vase with embossed design.*

Above. *Copper-luster pitcher with unusual hound spout.*

Above. *Silver-resist luster pitcher.*

Right. *Polychrome enamel bottle with conventional birds and flowers.* (Philadelphia Museum of Art)

Above. *Transfer-printed copper luster goblet.*

195

Pine desk with high open shelves. The space is partitioned in an orderly and interesting way. This aristocratic piece is earlier than those desks with wood doors that closed over the shelves. Manchester, Massachusetts.

with detachable hangers on their door counterparts were an early and delicate adaptation for inside-the-house furnishings of the strap or hanger hinge used for heavy door and gate use. Delicate butterfly hinges were namesakes of their obvious inspiration. These are difficult to come by, as is true of most early colonial forgings. Strap hinges, the better-known H and L hinges, and butterfly hinges all seem to have been a more popular design with the New England and coastal Colonies than with the interior farm settlements. During the early nineteenth century, door-hinge castings copied the slanted base of the forged farm-gate hinge pin, a novel idea for a self-closing gate worked by gravitation alone. It is still a good idea, particularly for

American Chippendale wing chair with straight legs. 1760–1775.

houses with children who rarely, if ever, close doors.

The latches, door handles, hasps, hinges, and various other forgings used to strengthen chests and carts were only some of the blacksmiths' products. Ironwork was forged for the huge Conestoga wagons that were used to transport goods across the country long before track had been laid for the railroads. These utilitarian pieces of early iron represent some of the colonial blacksmiths' finest efforts in decorative and practical forgings, comparable by any standards to the best forgings of any time or place.

When the uninitiated collector runs

Above. *Modest Queen Anne mirror with walnut veneering. 1700–1725.*

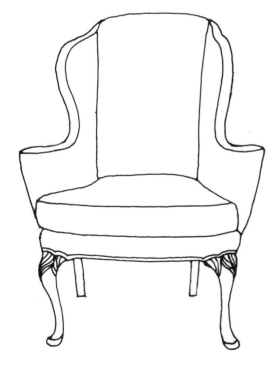

Above. *Early eighteenth century pine desk with maple frame employed the use of a molding plane. When open, the lid rests on nearly square arms.*

Left. *Queen Anne walnut wing chair. 1715.*

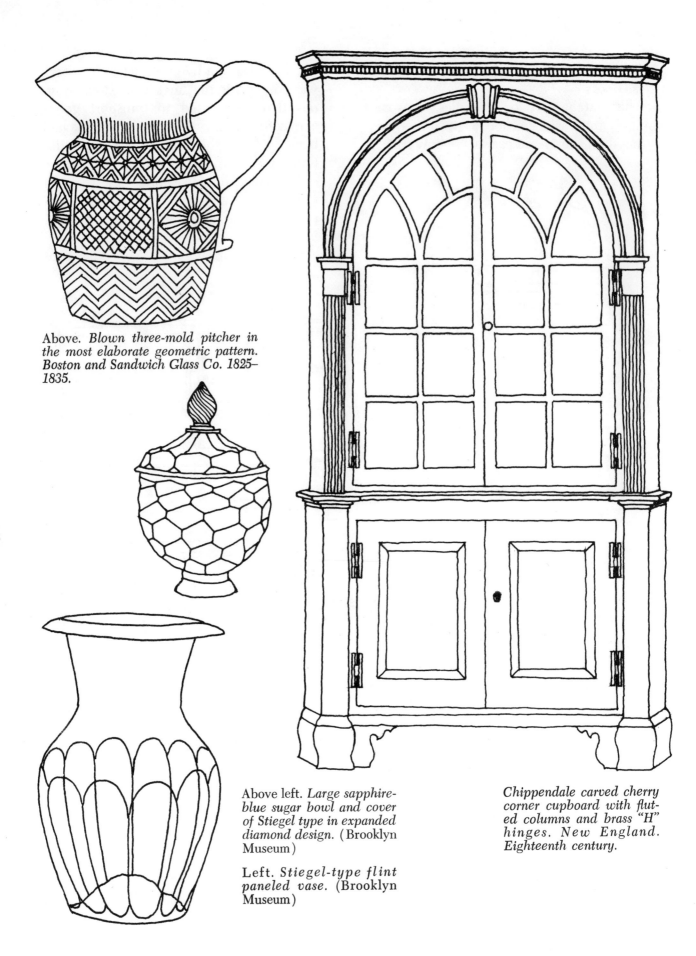

Above. *Blown three-mold pitcher in the most elaborate geometric pattern. Boston and Sandwich Glass Co. 1825–1835.*

Above left. *Large sapphire-blue sugar bowl and cover of Stiegel type in expanded diamond design.* (Brooklyn Museum)

Left. *Stiegel-type flint paneled vase.* (Brooklyn Museum)

Chippendale carved cherry corner cupboard with fluted columns and brass "H" hinges. New England. Eighteenth century.

across a primitive weather vane made of sheet iron, he is likely to be most surprised by its huge size and weight. When it is perched high on top of a house or barn and observed from below, its size is quite deceiving. Cut out of sheet iron or copper or sometimes cast in a wafer-thin mold, they more often portray barnyard animals than any other subject. Silhouetted against the sky, their forms are both attractive and useful, for in spite of their weight and size and primitive construction, they are balanced to turn with the wind easily and to dependably pass on the information they were made to give. On the coastal areas of New England where weather is of vital importance to the sea-going population, the weather vanes were cut in shapes depicting objects that were an integral part of the seaman's life at that time: silhouettes of ships in full sail, whales—so vital to the industry of those early ports—porpoises, sea gulls, and the ever-present arrows pointing the way to the four corners of the world.

When one sees a snow-scraper on the front porch of a suburban home, it is interesting to remember that it had no such elegant positioning in the past. Its original function was, in fact, most inelegant: It was set in the stone step at the back door to be used for the ignominious chore of removing barn manure from the boots

Above top. *Sugar bowl with lilypad decoration. 1800–1850.* Above bottom. *Blown glass pitcher in a lilypad style characteristic of New York glasshouses during the 1831–1870 period.*

Left. *Pink flask of brilliant light green non-lead glass. American eagle on one side; on the reverse a large cornucopia coiled to left and filled with produce. Pittsburgh-Monongahela district. 1820–1824.*

Opposite page: top left. *Tin candle mold for making ten candles.* Bottom left. *Rushlight holder of wrought iron.*

Below. *Tin mold for making six tall slender candles.*

Revolutionary War–period serpentine desk made of pine and painted to imitate another wood. The top section drops forward on quarter-circle brass supports; when closed the piece looks like a chest of drawers.

of the farm help before they tracked up the well-scrubbed floor of the kitchen. Wrought-iron scrapers did "graduate" to the front of the house rather early in colonial times. However, the original purpose did not change, for they were now stationed at the front door to scrape the boots of the gentry arriving by horse. Of course, in New England, where the snows are heavy and the spring mud a problem for the housewife, the small iron forgings served a double duty. In any case, snowscrapers are still with us; they are decorative and perfectly appropriate by the front door, even though they are no longer waiting to help someone who has gone to fetch some milk or eggs from the barn and is bound to return to the kitchen.

There are many less familiar forged or cast items that were a part of the daily life of the settler. Though the use to which they were originally put is no longer pressing, they are a fascinating part of our history. The bootjack was designed to make the removing of one's boots a one-man job, freeing one's wife or servant from the chore. The simple idea of placing one's foot on the jack to hold it to the floor, and placing the heel of the other boot between the jack's arms, made it quite easy to slip off the boot. The bootjacks were always V-shaped and were used by most of the men of the time, humble or wealthy. These useful irons could be cast or forged in any shape, as long as the design could be adapted to the function: insects with sturdy antennae, naughty nude ladies with their legs outstretched, and a myriad of geometrical forms. As long as

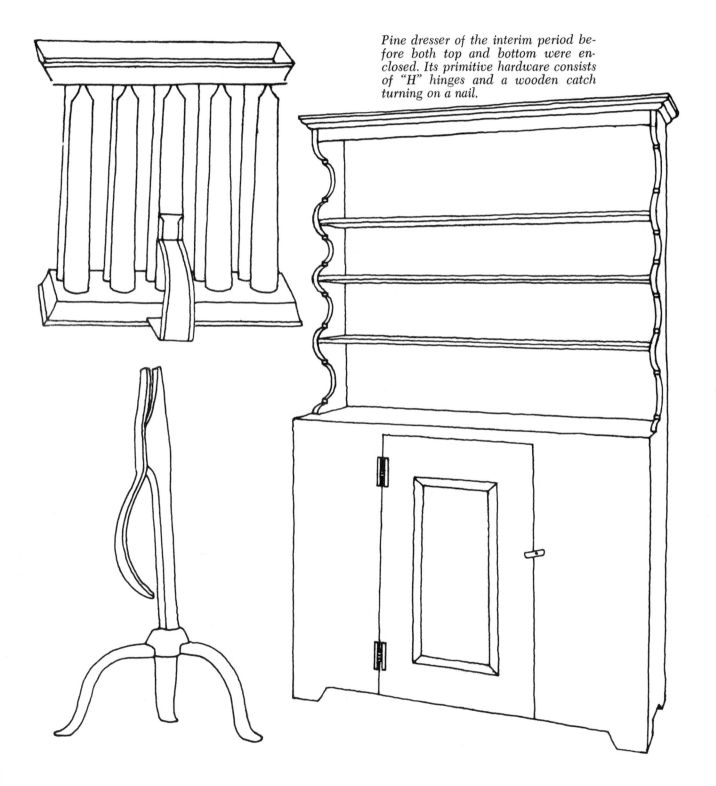

Pine dresser of the interim period before both top and bottom were enclosed. Its primitive hardware consists of "H" hinges and a wooden catch turning on a nail.

they performed their task, the castings designer at the furnace or the blacksmith at the forge could let his imagination go wild. Entertaining in form, they are highly prized by those collectors interested in small forgings and castings.

Just as an aside, because of the present popularity of long boots for the ladies in

Below. *Massachusetts pine desk with cabinet top, solid doors. Every part of this piece is heavily constructed and though lacking in delicacy it is consistent, and its proportions are pleasing.*

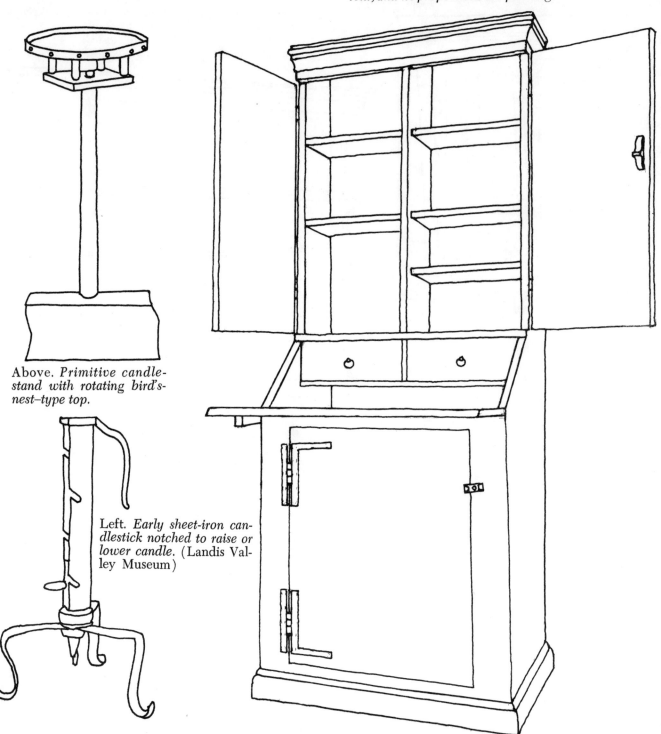

Above. *Primitive candlestand with rotating bird's-nest–type top.*

Left. *Early sheet-iron candlestick notched to raise or lower candle.* (Landis Valley Museum)

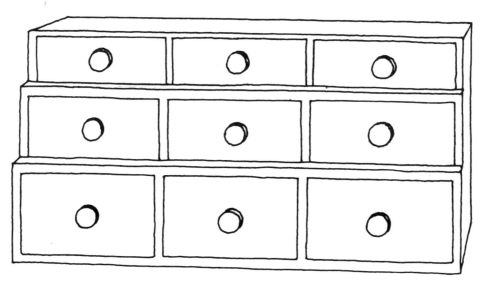

A set of spice boxes designed to sit on a shelf or table rather than to hang on a wall.

the winter, the bootjack may enjoy a renewal of popularity along with the equally ancient, but still very much in use, shoehorn.

Another interesting cast item dates the popularity and availability of string or twine, a commodity so taken for granted now. Although jute was used for rope from the time there were boats with sails, its use as a daily convenience is most recent. Twine made of cotton was very costly and was used over and over again. As it became more available, it was used in general stores for exactly the same purpose that it is now used, the difference being that it was contained in a decorative cast-iron ball of open-work design that hung from the ceiling of the store directly over the service counter for all the customers to see.

Pennsylvania pine water bench with scrolled top and three drawers.

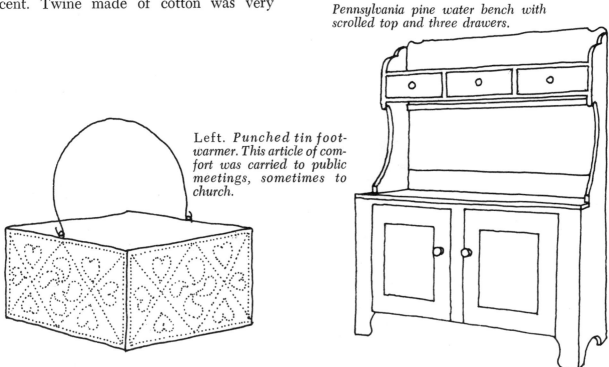

Left. *Punched tin foot-warmer. This article of comfort was carried to public meetings, sometimes to church.*

Tall clock or grandfather clock by Aaron Willard. 1800.

Ashel Cheney tall clock. Northfield, Massachusetts. 1790.

THE HALL

Clocks should be thought of as something more than furniture, certainly more than decorations. Clocks are really members of the family. Perhaps this is because their presence is continuously heard as well as seen. They give accurate information when we need it. They are trust-

worthy, they are steady, uncomplaining, and demand very little in the way of attention and care. In fact, they perform just as good friends should. Clocks have a long history. Handed down from generation to generation, they are valued, if not as accurate timepieces, then for the antique

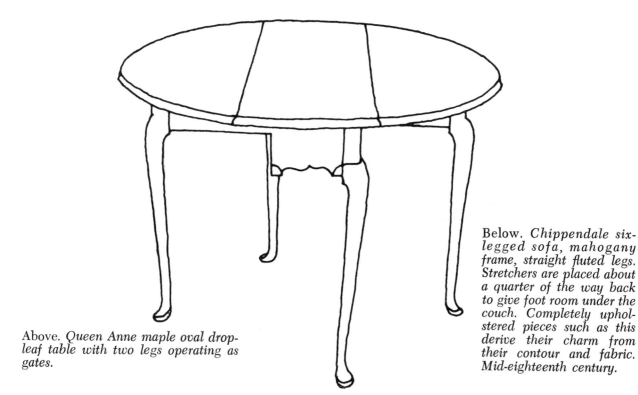

Above. *Queen Anne maple oval drop-leaf table with two legs operating as gates.*

Below. *Chippendale six-legged sofa, mahogany frame, straight fluted legs. Stretchers are placed about a quarter of the way back to give foot room under the couch. Completely upholstered pieces such as this derive their charm from their contour and fabric. Mid-eighteenth century.*

beauty that is so prized by the decorator. We have never heard of a clock in a wood case ever having been thrown away. There is something about the sound of a clock that stirs inner emotions and conjures up recollections of the past. Perhaps they recall the one town clock that was such a significant part of our ancestors' lives. The inside workings of a clock usually designated the form of the case. According

to the experts, pendulum clocks date back to the middle 1600's. This clock's long case was necessary in order to protect the pendulum's delicately balanced swing from dust and windy drafts.

History reminds us of an interesting fact concerning this "member of the family." Almost everyone of importance during our colonial times owned a clock. It is also a fact that an extremely high per-

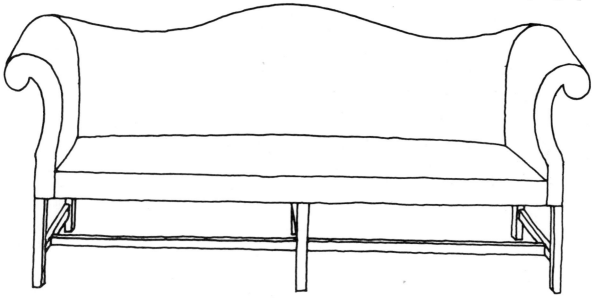

centage of those particular clocks can be seen in museums and in private collections. They are important, not only for themselves, but because they played such a vital part in the daily lives of their impressive owners. Famous and influential historical personages consulted with these very clocks all during the day, as we do the same with our timepieces now. Clocks are not just a symbol of the past; they made an active contribution at a time when our history was in the making. A clock is truly ageless; although its case or works may be of a style or fashion of one particular time, its function is the same—past, present, and future.

Maybe there are so many fine clocks still in existence because they were a vitally important need and offered intelligent

Above, and below left. *Victorian gentleman's armchair and lady's chair with low small arms, typical of American factory-made work between 1860 and 1875.*

Chippendale mahogany Pembroke table has one small drop leaf and becomes a square when leaf is raised. 1750.

Above. *Small Hepplewhite filigree mir-ror. 1780–1790.*

Left and right. *Victorian hanging hall lamps. Globes are ruby glass and spiral opal glass, fittings are brass.*

assistance to their owners. Usually they reposed in places safe from harm, another reason for their excellent state of preservation.

Most clocks of impressive historic value were the products of two master craftsmen: The works were made by clockmakers, the beautiful cases were created by the finest cabinetmakers. Mahogany, walnut, and pine were used for the cases and in some extraordinary clocks, marquetry and handsome lacquer work was also applied. The dials on the faces were often considered works of art and the faces were engraved in brass, chased, enameled, and decorated with motifs of the seasons, cherubs, or garlands of finely painted flowers. Indeed, subjects for dec-

Right. *Little New England half-round table of pine, with three legs.*

Above. *Candlestick blown from aquamarine glass. 1862.*

Above. *Blown candlestick of clear non-lead glass. Pennsylvania. Eighteenth century.*

Left. *Tall blown candlestick, column of shaft with a central air twist. Pittsburgh area. 1815–1830.*

orating and embellishing were myriad: bucolic landscapes, birds in flight, and ships at sea were several of the most popular.

Occasionally, depending on the whim of the clockmaker and his genius for mechanical effects, little animated figures would appear on the dial to express the time of day or night.

A study of the workmanship of the hands of antique clocks is fascinating because of the variety of creative effort exerted on this single feature. In the detail of the hands alone one can trace the history of clockmaking in the Colonies. Clockmakers were much in demand and could be found turning out their varied products from New England, south to Virginia and west to Ohio, from as early as 1685 until around 1850. "After 1850 the manufacturing of clocks changed from the special and made-to-order clock to the more or less mass-produced clock." Copies of fine old English clocks rivaled the best products of English makers, and the cases made in America were difficult to distinguish from the better known cabinetmakers' cases made in Europe. When Eli Terry, of Connecticut, introduced his famous pillar-and-scroll mantel or shelf clock, he set the fashion in short pendulum clocks for all time. At the same time, early in the nineteenth century, Seth Thomas, Simon Willard, and Elias Ingraham were also making clocks that are still highly prized by all collectors and home decorators.

The banjo clock of the 1800's, a style brought out by Simon Willard of Boston, challenged the popularity of the grandfather clock or tall clock, popular for so many years. The painted glass door of the base of the tall clock was covered with illustrations of a variety of subjects: landscapes, naval scenes, and patriotic decorations, to name a few. The more elaborately decorated clocks of this style are attributed to Aaron Willard, the brother of Simon.

One can learn from reading early advertisements that there were varieties of clocks for sale as early as 1795: eight-day clocks with chimes, musical clocks, clocks with ornamented figures, and many others. Even that early in our history, clocks were well on their way to becoming a necessary household item. On the subject

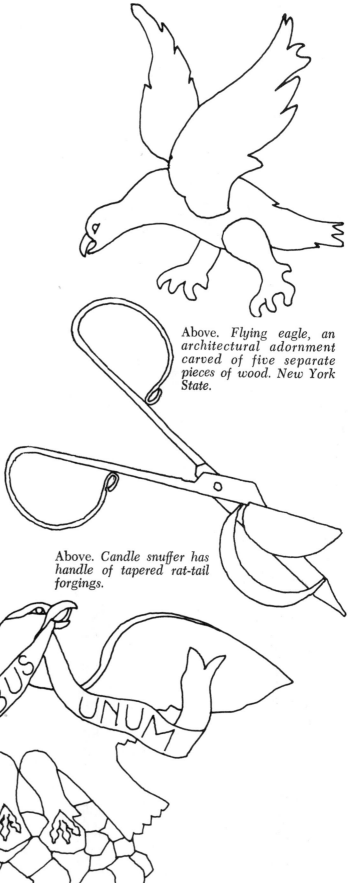

Above. *Flying eagle, an architectural adornment carved of five separate pieces of wood. New York State.*

Above. *Candle snuffer has handle of tapered rat-tail forgings.*

Polychromed sternboard eagle carved from a single piece of pine has a wingspread of forty-eight inches. Found near Salem, Massachusetts. Nineteenth century.

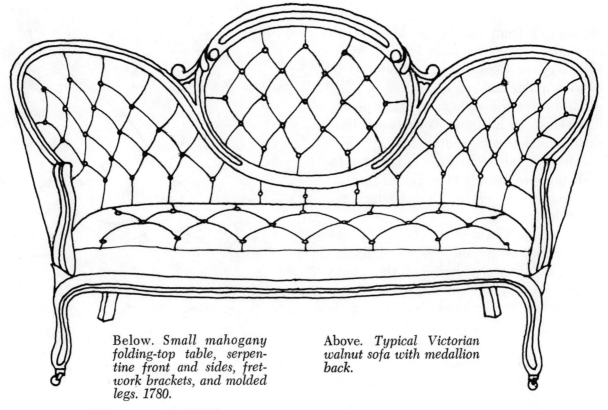

Above. *Typical Victorian walnut sofa with medallion back.*

Below. *Small mahogany folding-top table, serpentine front and sides, fretwork brackets, and molded legs. 1780.*

of productivity, however, there is no doubt that Connecticut produced more than its share of both clockmakers and their handsome products and held this distinguished position for many years. We illustrate many of the most popular clocks of those early times, but it must be remembered that clockmakers went on, long after the period of the classic and made-to-order clocks, to continue their work making an infinite variety of styles and cases.

Few of the finer American clocks are to be found outside of museums or the better private collections. There are, however, many fascinating early and late Victorian clocks of all shapes, case styles, and colors that are still not difficult to find in shops and at auctions. Fortunately, they are not yet prohibitive in price. They may not be as accurate as timepieces should be and their chimes are not nearly as melodious as those of their more classic predecessors, but as charming wall and mantel pieces, they are as full of nostalgia and decorating pleasure as their venerated forerunners. We must remind you that in

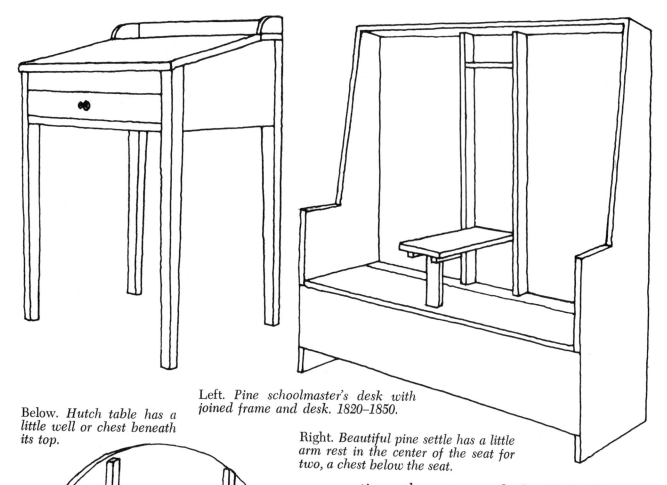

Below. *Hutch table has a little well or chest beneath its top.*

Left. *Pine schoolmaster's desk with joined frame and desk. 1820–1850.*

Right. *Beautiful pine settle has a little arm rest in the center of the seat for two, a chest below the seat.*

time, they, too, undoubtedly will take their proper place as early Americana and their value is likely to increase correspondingly.

An added and sometimes unexpected bonus found in many early Connecticut clocks was the printed advertisement and direction sheet on how to use and repair the clock. This printed sheet was mounted on the inside back of the clock's case. These fascinating woodcuts or lithographs of the manufacturer's directions and warranties are highly prized, indeed. In cases where the clock itself has been destroyed but the back panel with its printed matter is still intact, the panel or the sheet alone may be framed to make both an interesting bit of antiquity and a delightful wall decoration. Among dealers, to be considered in mint condition, a clock must still have this printed sheet intact and attached to the inside case just as

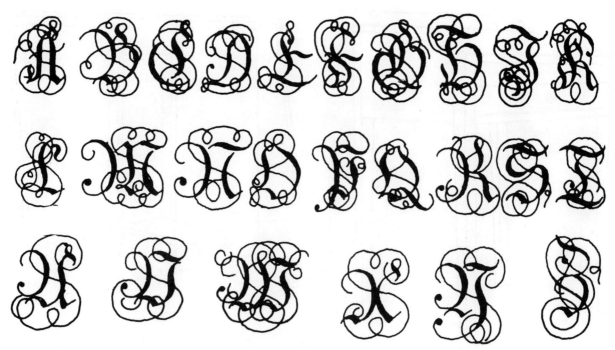

Old fractur alphabet.

it was originally sold by the manufacturer.

Because clock designs have always followed the popular ideas of the times, clocks were made to commemorate the historic events of this country. A very popular subject was the sinking of the *Maine* during the attack on Havana Harbor in Teddy Roosevelt's time. These commemorative clock cases were mostly cast in brass and depicted the historic event in many different sculptured arrangements. The one thing all these mass-produced clocks had in common was an excessively patriotic view of the Spanish-American War, which was thoroughly in accord with the mood of the country. Although these exuberant commemorative clocks will hardly replace the lovely Chippendale

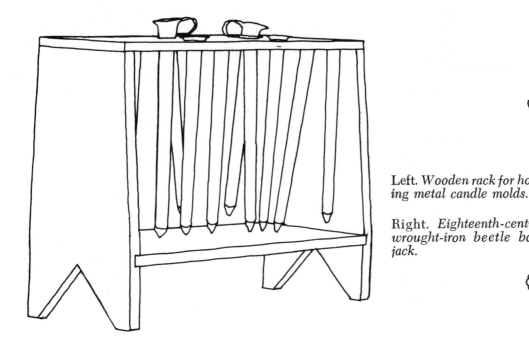

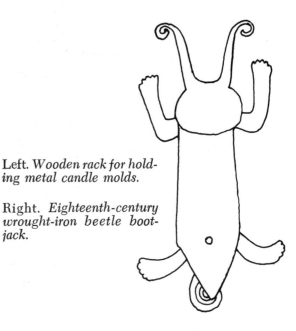

Left. *Wooden rack for holding metal candle molds.*

Right. *Eighteenth-century wrought-iron beetle bootjack.*

Steel-engraved baptismal certificate with fractur. Dated 1824.

masterpieces in museum clock collections, as time goes on they are bound to become of ever-increasing interest and value to owners and collectors. An added attraction: The modern viewer is likely to find the mantel clocks' larger-than-life interpretation of historic and patriotic subjects delightfully amusing.

The single most important influence on decorating with antiques, particularly in the living room area, is the light. Although modern artificial light is quite simple to adjust according to the overall effect desired, the windows are quite another thing. As the only source of natural light in a room, little thought is generally given to their decorative advantages.

To wish that the windows were larger,

Baptismal certificate, lithographed on stone and hand painted. Fractur. Dated 1827.

a little more to the right or to the left, higher or lower, is certainly the decorator's privilege, but to take advantage of the decorating potential of these rarely perfectly placed fixtures takes a bit of know-how. Antiques always look better when the light is of the quality of their original settings. In early New England houses, wall construction was only as thick as the two-inch, feather-edged, exterior vertical planking, and the hand-planed panel boards that became the walls of the interior of the room. The wall thickness usually totaled no more than four to five inches and so the windows were shallow in depth. Consequently, the inside win-

Steel-engraved baptismal certificate,
printed in four colors. Fractur. Dated
1849.

dow sills were quite narrow.

The lights or small panes of glass set in the delicate wood mullions of the sash were often imperfect by our standards for window glass today. The glass was likely to have a pale violet hue, a charming color that has, unfortunately, been eliminated by progress in the present-day process of window glass making. Of course, bubbly antique window glass magnifies and distorts the view outside and is not an aid in accurately viewing the landscape, but, after all, how much time does one spend staring out the window with a need for 20/20 detail?

Often the construction detail of the inside window sills was continued as a molding level with the sills all around the room. This formed the chair rail, a characteristic of the interior woodwork of many early houses. In panel-lined frame houses, the chair rail separated the vertical panels, which rose from the rail to the ceiling beam, from the horizontal panels, which went from the chair rail to the floor. Both vertical and horizontal panels, as well as the chair-rail molding itself, varied in design from the most simple form of woodwork in primitive houses to grand paneling and beautiful handmade moldings in the more elegant houses.

Because the stone walls of the Pennsylvania Dutch country houses were constructed some twenty to thirty inches in thickness, the window sills were extremely deep on the inside and admitted much less light into the room than did the thinner-walled New England windows. Thus, while

Below. *Majolica pitcher, raised sunflower design on both sides, pewter top, made in Pennsylvania. American majolica was also made in Baltimore, Trenton, Ohio, New York, and New Hampshire from 1880 to 1892.*

Left. *Pine corner shelves. Both the side boards and the shelves are scrolled with graceful curves.*

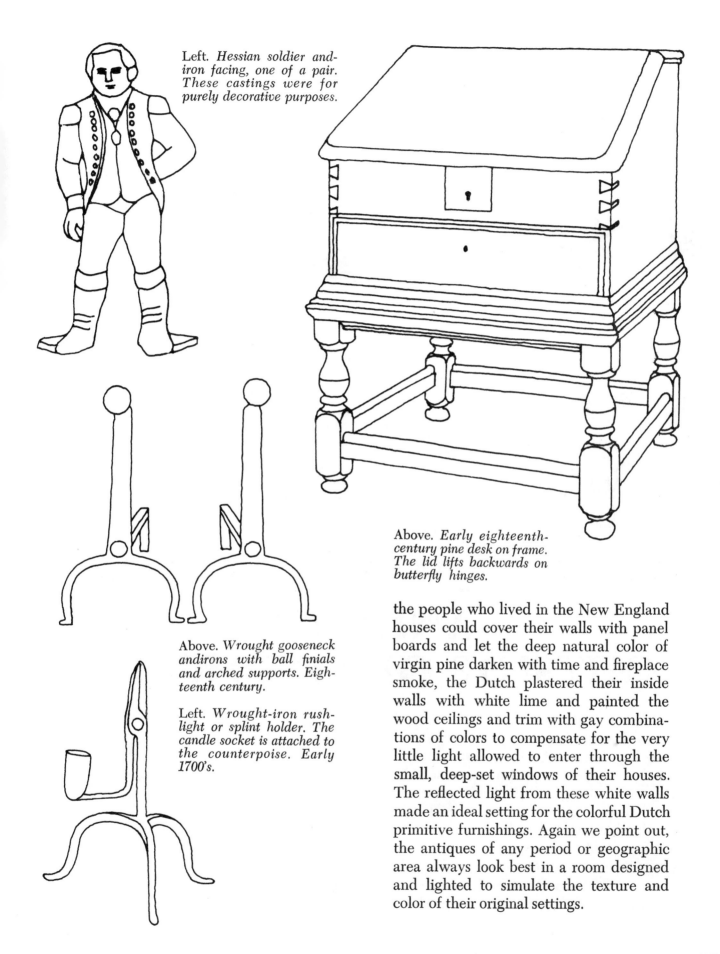

Left. *Hessian soldier andiron facing, one of a pair. These castings were for purely decorative purposes.*

Above. *Early eighteenth-century pine desk on frame. The lid lifts backwards on butterfly hinges.*

Above. *Wrought gooseneck andirons with ball finials and arched supports. Eighteenth century.*

Left. *Wrought-iron rush-light or splint holder. The candle socket is attached to the counterpoise. Early 1700's.*

the people who lived in the New England houses could cover their walls with panel boards and let the deep natural color of virgin pine darken with time and fireplace smoke, the Dutch plastered their inside walls with white lime and painted the wood ceilings and trim with gay combinations of colors to compensate for the very little light allowed to enter through the small, deep-set windows of their houses. The reflected light from these white walls made an ideal setting for the colorful Dutch primitive furnishings. Again we point out, the antiques of any period or geographic area always look best in a room designed and lighted to simulate the texture and color of their original settings.

Pennsylvania Dutch settee, heavily constructed in every detail. Its double chest was probably used for storing wood in the kitchen. The three back braces are scrolled in the popular tulip design. 1830.

THE PORCH, THE TERRACE, AND THE OUTSIDE OF THE HOUSE

The porch is another structural feature that has been refined over the years. They were nonexistent in most of the Cape Cod and New England constructions, because by the time they had finished a day's work, people had had about all they could take of the outdoors. There were, however, spendidly oversized and formal porches on the Southern Colonial structures. Those pillared and spacious

façades were not designed to protect the user from flies, mosquitos, and the other insects that have always tortured porch or patio users. Terraces of the early times, when they existed at all, were likely to resemble *palazzos* overlooking the Rhine or Mediterranean. Some beautiful and simple brick-paved ones were built in and around the central colonies of Maryland and Virginia. These miniature gardens,

Right. *Pine lantern, painted red. Its top is hollowed out and domed to accommodate the perforated tin cap.*

Below. *Unique cock weathervane of sheet iron, 13½ inches high, three-dimensional construction.*

often secluded by magnificent boxwood hedges, provided comfort, privacy, and attractiveness that is adaptable to present outside-the-house-living requirements.

It must be remembered that in the early primitive days, cookouts were a necessity. The smokehouse and oven that were usually separated from the house by a few yards were vital to the household

cooking. Generally, they were placed so that they were easily accessible from the front door. There were no kitchen doors at that time, for the simple reason that there were no kitchens. Bread, beans, and baked goods that could be made in quan-

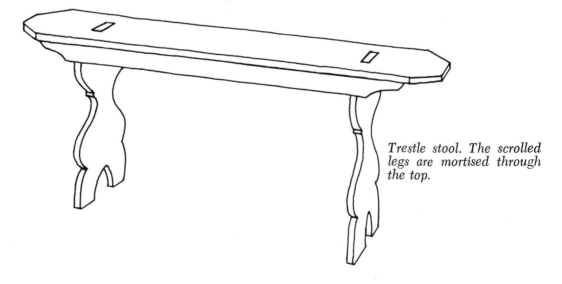

Trestle stool. The scrolled legs are mortised through the top.

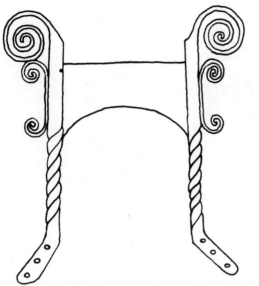

Above. *Ornamental wrought-iron boot scraper, twisted and scrolled forgings. Eighteenth century.*

tity were cooked in the outdoor oven. While the baking was going on, meat was preserved in the smokehouse, which used the same chimney and fuel. This took care of curing hams, bacon, and the types of sausage that called for smoke preservation. Summer kitchens, added to the original house at a slightly later period, were a luxury. Smokehouses continued their useful function late into the nineteenth century.

With this history of cooking outside the house, it is not surprising that the re-

Below. *Pennsylvania Dutch dry sink with single knife drawer.*

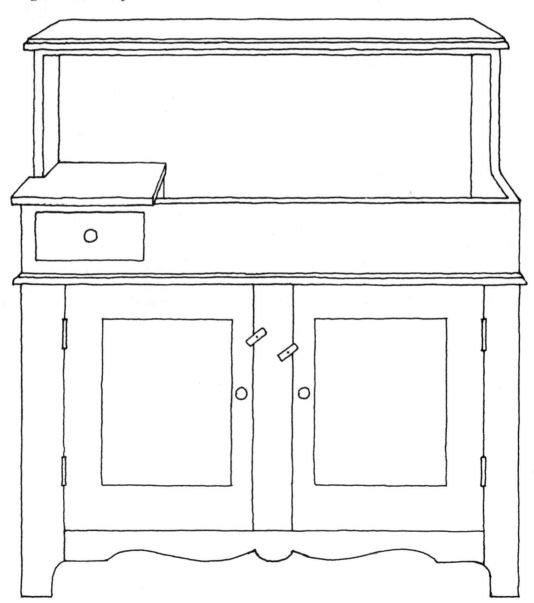

turn to outdoor cookery comes quite naturally to most of us. Arranging an attractive place for this highly acceptable cookout area is certainly a worthwhile venture. It is not necessary to make it a huge project, but there is no reason why the area for outdoor cooking cannot be attractive and at least partially in the early American style. It is appropriate, for the barbecue is basically just a fireplace outside of the house.

It is not necessary to build a brick or stone oven to imitate the structures of the past, but if you do, it will outlast many modern sheet-metal cookout gadgets and repay the effort many times over should you ultimately market your property.

Soft, bright orange brick is certainly available at any brickyard, for cheap common brick is still in use. If you prefer secondhand brick, which is likely to look more authentic, it is not difficult to obtain. When set tightly together in a pre-

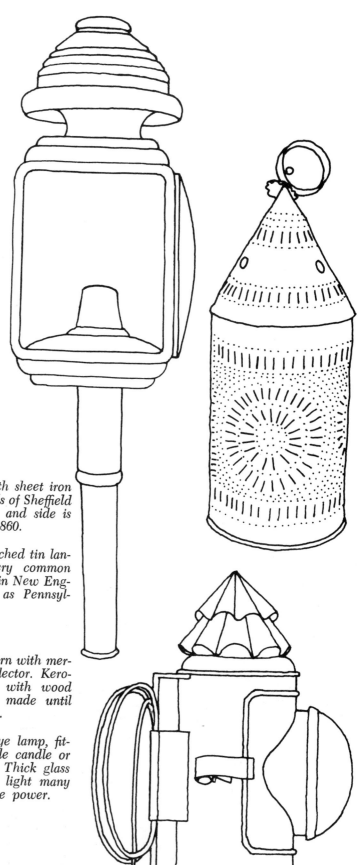

Right. Carriage lamp with sheet iron japanned black, and bands of Sheffield plate. Glass in the back and side is silvered to reflect light. 1860.

Far right. Punched tin lantern of a very common variety, made in New England as well as Pennsylvania.

Left. Tin lantern with mercury glass reflector. Kerosene lanterns with wood handles were made until the mid-1800's.

Right. Bull's-eye lamp, fitted for a single candle or tiny oil fount. Thick glass lens magnifies light many times its feeble power.

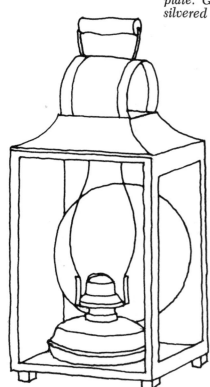

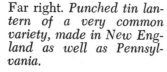

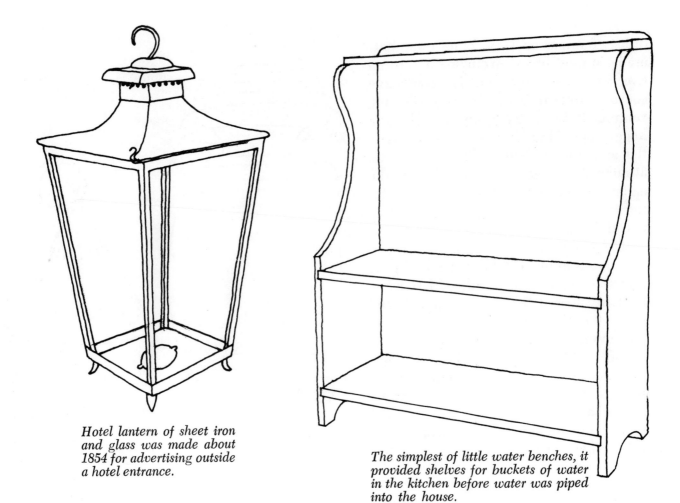

Hotel lantern of sheet iron and glass was made about 1854 for advertising outside a hotel entrance.

The simplest of little water benches, it provided shelves for buckets of water in the kitchen before water was piped into the house.

pared sand base, the brick oven looks just as antique and functions just as well as the original ovens.

Old seats, butchers' benches, outdoor lanterns, and cooking irons can all be used to decorate the cookout area, for basically that is where many of these items really belong. Long-handled shovels used to remove the bread or beans baking deep in the oven, iron and copper apple butter and scalding kettles—almost any utensil that was a part of the outdoor equipment in the early days is useful and looks right in the outdoor living areas today.

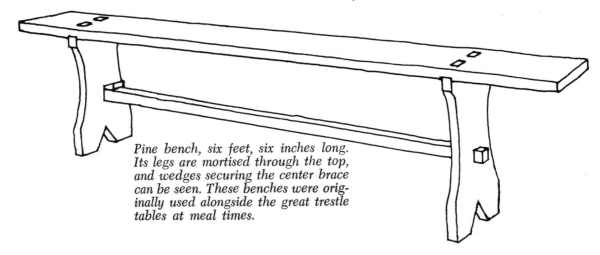

Pine bench, six feet, six inches long. Its legs are mortised through the top, and wedges securing the center brace can be seen. These benches were originally used alongside the great trestle tables at meal times.

In the summer when the terrace or porch is so practical for entertaining, the lamps and planters of colonial times will add another delightful touch for they will be performing the exact duties they were originally made for.

Another popular and familiar article of furniture that had a curious early development is the desk. Although the desk is still not an absolutely essential piece of furniture, everyone has a cardboard or metal box in which to store bills, papers, correspondence, receipts, and the myriad written communications that clutter our lives. Well, that box is where the desk started.

Originally called a "desk box," it was a primitive six-board box with staple hinges and a few partitions where the more pre-

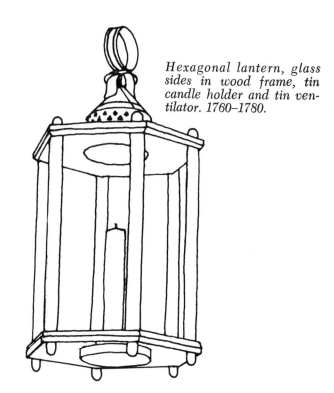

Hexagonal lantern, glass sides in wood frame, tin candle holder and tin ventilator. 1760–1780.

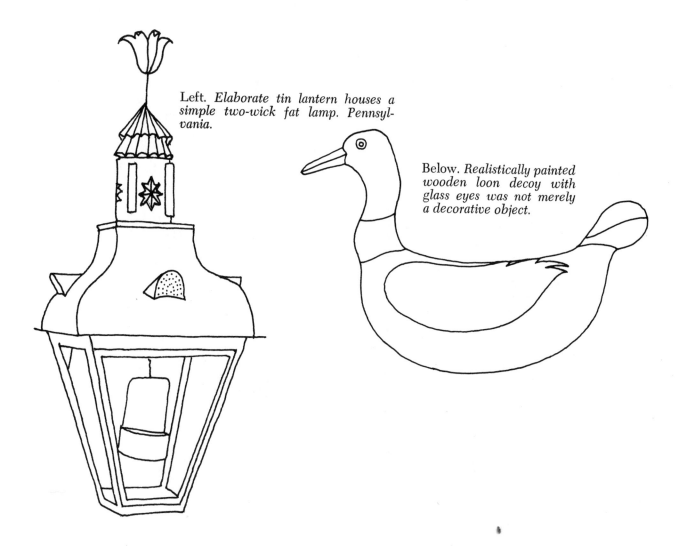

Left. *Elaborate tin lantern houses a simple two-wick fat lamp. Pennsylvania.*

Below. *Realistically painted wooden loon decoy with glass eyes was not merely a decorative object.*

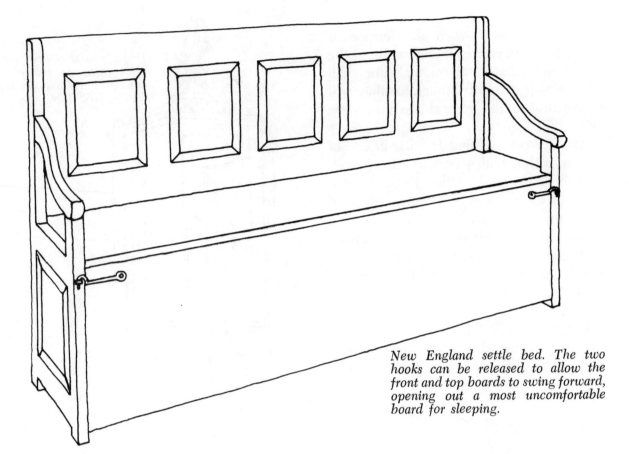

New England settle bed. The two hooks can be released to allow the front and top boards to swing forward, opening out a most uncomfortable board for sleeping.

cious papers were stored. Later this box was constructed as part of a table, a convenience for those who needed to refer to its contents often and wanted to sit down while doing so. The box got larger as storage needs became greater until finally

it covered the table's total surface. Later it developed a slant top to make writing on it easier. It was only a matter of time before someone decided to reverse the hinged top from back to front so that the inside surface could then become the

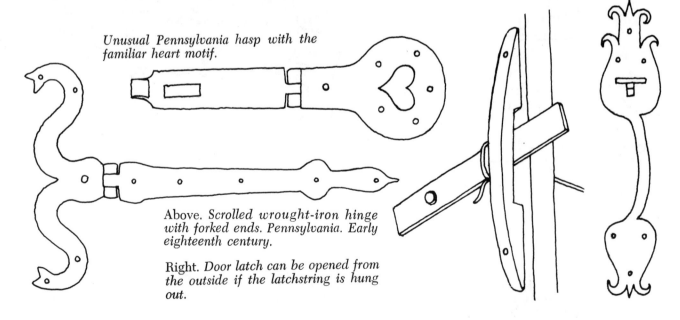

Unusual Pennsylvania hasp with the familiar heart motif.

Above. *Scrolled wrought-iron hinge with forked ends. Pennsylvania. Early eighteenth century.*

Right. *Door latch can be opened from the outside if the latchstring is hung out.*

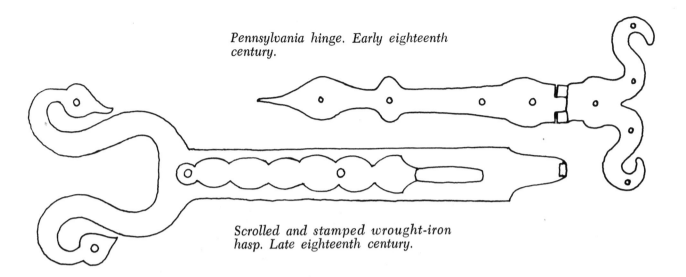

Pennsylvania hinge. Early eighteenth century.

Scrolled and stamped wrought-iron hasp. Late eighteenth century.

writing surface and, at the same time, the contents of the box were readily accessible for reference. The heavy pull-out supports on which the top rested became slender and the original table on which the box rested became part of the actual construction of the desk box. The slant top now projected forward sufficiently to give the user leg room. Finally, the open table construction under the writing surface was replaced first with one drawer, then with drawers right down to the floor. The vertical partitions in the box developed into the now familiar horizontal

Wrought-iron door latches: Opposite page, bottom right. Tulip design. Below. Two ball-and-spear latches, heart, tulip bud, and triangle designs.

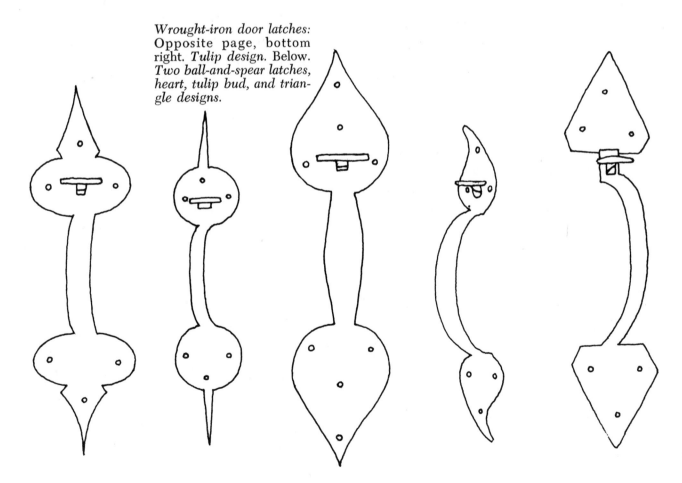

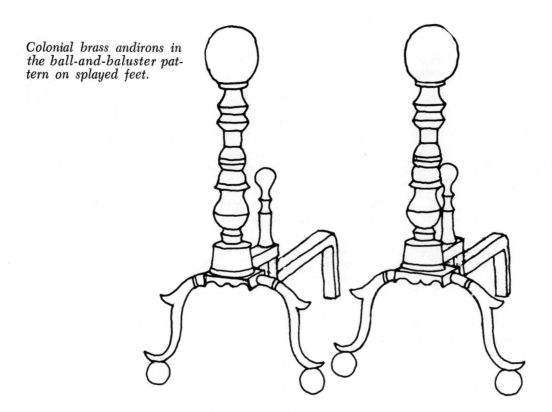

Colonial brass andirons in the ball-and-baluster pattern on splayed feet.

pigeonholes, complete with separate tiny drawers and secret cubbyholes. This arrangement became so large and complex that eventually glass-doored cabinets for the storage of books and *objets d'art* were constructed with the desk as its base. If you do not own a desk, we strongly urge you to abandon your battered old cardboard box, and give a desk a try. We are sure that its practicality and convenience will convince you that the long development from humble box to sophisticated furnishing was well worthwhile (and may

even help keep your accounts in order). Aside from the utilitarian values of a desk, it is without doubt one of the most attractive pieces to own. From a decorative standpoint, it looks right in either the living room or the den, and can easily be used as a hall piece.

Coffee tables, a comparatively recent living-room furnishing, also have their roots in the past; they are an adaptation of the butler's tray, a portable wooden stand with small folding sides, much in use in Victorian times. The butler's tray

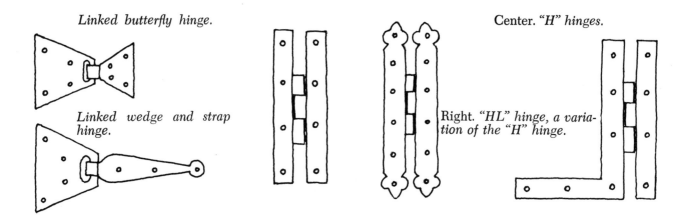

Linked butterfly hinge.

Linked wedge and strap hinge.

Center. "H" hinges.

Right. "HL" hinge, a variation of the "H" hinge.

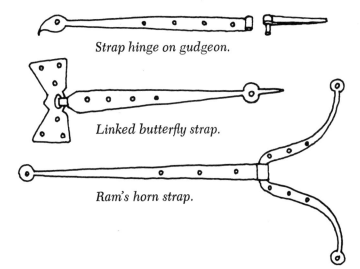

Strap hinge on gudgeon.

Linked butterfly strap.

Ram's horn strap.

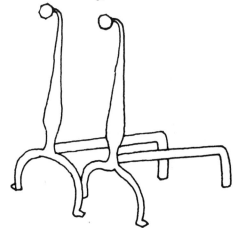

Small wrought-iron andirons made by a blacksmith in Salisbury, Connecticut.

is still quite acceptable as a coffee table today. In fact, there are many antiques that are readily adaptable to this present-day use. Victorian marble-top tables cut down to a useful size or surfaces of polished wood supported by iron stands are ideal. Dutch pallets or more primitive benches are wide and low and, when well refinished, will not give away their more prosaic pasts, except, perhaps, as conver-

sation pieces. During the 1920's the cobbler's bench was king of the coffee tables.

When one touches on the subject of chairs for comfort, the elimination of many American styles must take place. The ladder or slat-back chairs of the early New England Colonies are strictly for looking, not sitting, but as collectors' items there is always a place for them. The simple plank-seated chairs of a slightly later period are, however, most comfortable, practical, and almost indestructible. Hitchcock, balloon-back, half-spindle, and many other chairs also fit into this category. If they still have their original paint and decal decoration, you

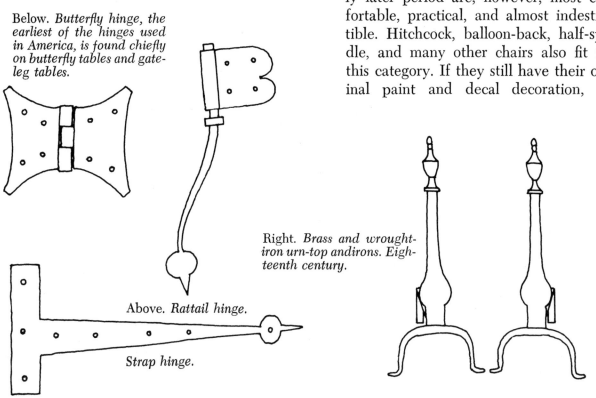

Below. *Butterfly hinge, the earliest of the hinges used in America, is found chiefly on butterfly tables and gate-leg tables.*

Above. *Rattail hinge.*

Strap hinge.

Right. *Brass and wrought-iron urn-top andirons. Eighteenth century.*

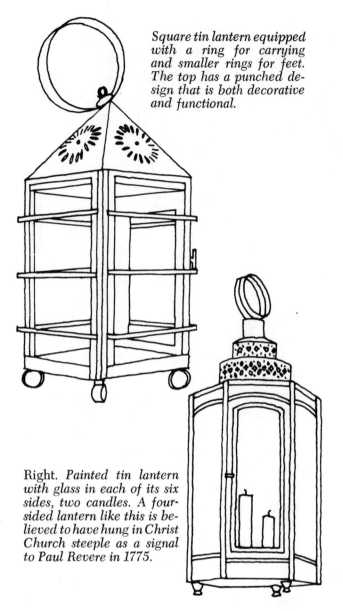

Square tin lantern equipped with a ring for carrying and smaller rings for feet. The top has a punched design that is both decorative and functional.

Right. *Painted tin lantern with glass in each of its six sides, two candles. A four-sided lantern like this is believed to have hung in Christ Church steeple as a signal to Paul Revere in 1775.*

would be well advised to let them add their color and charm to the room but to use them as utilitarian pieces only when necessary. Windsors are almost always a welcome addition to any home.

In the early colonial days upholstered chairs were owned exclusively by the well-to-do. They were beautifully made, handsomely covered, and taken care of carefully. As such, when found for sale outside of museums, they tend to be rather costly. The later Victorian and Empire periods made available to the less financially advantaged countless upholstered seats with, we must add, great variation in comfortableness. Some Victorian sofas or medallion-back seats are far more attractive than they are comfortable. People in those days sat up straight, at least in the parlor, and it was a valuable habit, for to slump down in one of those period pieces was uncomfortable and was not

Right. *Wooden lantern with tin bottom and top. On the wooden door in the rear are three mirror reflectors.*

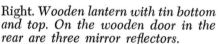

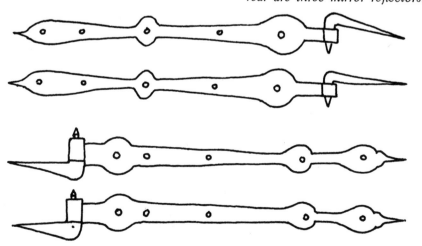

Left. *Iron door hinges of the early eighteenth century.*

Far right. *Weathervane cut out of sheet iron in the shape of a galloping horse.*

Below. *Painted codfish, one foot, six inches long, carved out of a 1¼-inch pine board.*

Bottom. *Butterfly weathervane, cut from sheet copper, hammered and pierced and mounted on horizontal and vertical rods. Late nineteenth century.*

Below. *Graceful rooster weathervane, cut out of sheet iron for the roof of a Pennsylvania house.*

considered genteel. Besides, the buttons of the tufting and the stabs from strands of the horsehair upholstery material were added hazards to one's anatomy. Today, the excellent upholstery materials and skills available make it easy to convert almost any of these uncomfortable furnishings into comfortable and colorful pieces. As long as the frames are made with well-

designed lines and the finish of the wood is in good condition, they can provide comfort to you and ever-increasing value to your collection.

In the early days of New England, when one wanted to lock a door from the inside he would fit the end of a heavy beam of hard maple into a slot provided in the doorframe. The end of the beam would rest in a saddle of wood or forged iron on the other side of the door. When all this was accomplished, it would be difficult for anyone to enter without first being invited, at which time the entire action had to be reversed. Unhappily, this kind of protection was only useful when there were people at home. Of course, the earliest colonists had nothing in the way of luxuries, and locks were to protect the

This delightful mermaid weathervane carved from one piece of pine with separate arms and metal mirror once floated over a barn in Wayland, Massachusetts. (Shelburne Museum, Shelburne, Vermont)

people in the house, not their possessions. However, as the Colonies became more "civilized" and the people began to accumulate things that were not just the bare necessities of life, it became necessary for people to lock their houses when they were not at home.

Drawing on the accumulated knowledge of locksmiths who had been acquainted with this same problem in most European countries, the colonials began to adapt, invent, and manufacture locks of iron to suit every purpose. Among other varieties, they developed crab locks on chests that took a sturdy key and a strong wrist to turn, and thumb latches that could be locked from the inside and outside of the door.

The massive door latch or spring latch found on doors of Pennsylvania Dutch houses had a heavy shot bolt in addition to its spring bolt making it almost identical in construction to the most modern door locks. Shot bolts varied in weight and

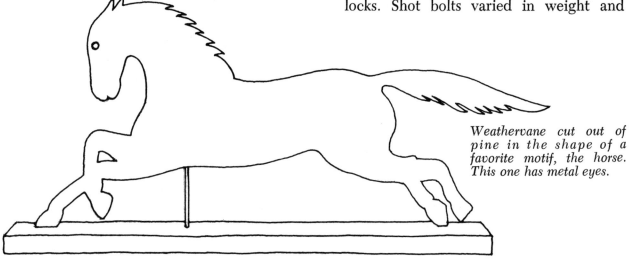

Weathervane cut out of pine in the shape of a favorite motif, the horse. This one has metal eyes.

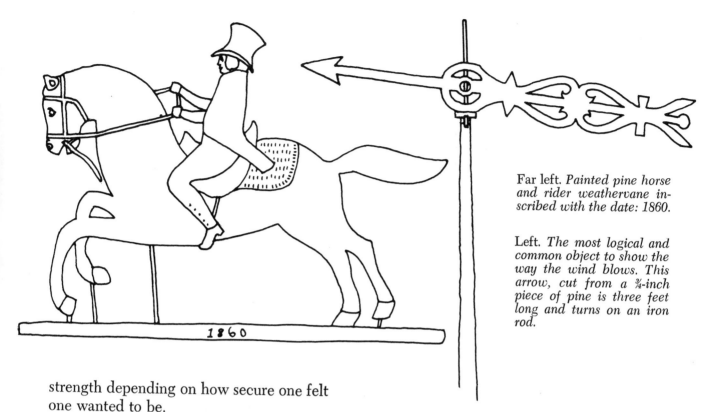

Far left. *Painted pine horse and rider weathervane inscribed with the date: 1860.*

Left. *The most logical and common object to show the way the wind blows. This arrow, cut from a ¾-inch piece of pine is three feet long and turns on an iron rod.*

strength depending on how secure one felt one wanted to be.

The colonial's life created a great need for lanterns, for his work kept him busy well into the night. Glass was costly and hard to come by, so the ingenious tinsmith constructed primitive lanterns of punched tin. These punchings were made in geometric patterns and the amount of light permitted through the perforations was barely adequate.

Lanterns were in general use throughout the Colonies and were usually constructed in the familiar cylindrical shape, topped with a cone-shaped cap to which a handle, also of tin, was attached. As glass became cheaper and easier to get, it was only a matter of time before these impractical sources of light were cast aside. They are still, however, most attractive when used in or near the outdoor areas

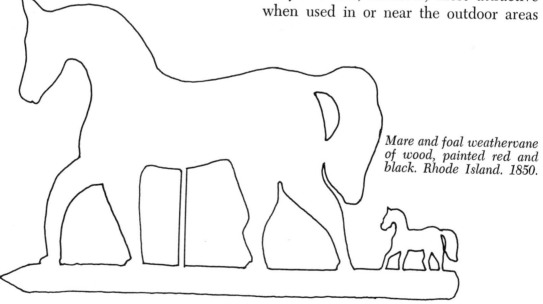

Mare and foal weathervane of wood, painted red and black. Rhode Island. 1850.

for which they were originally designed.

In conclusion, if we were to add a subhead to the title of this book, it would have to be a "how to" title. We believe that if you have learned "How to Be Fearless" in your decorating, we will have accomplished what we set out to do.

The experts on antiques are often so dedicated to either a single subject or to the original pure forms of each category of antiques that it is no surprise that the readers of their writings are intimidated unless they are already experienced collectors and make use of their collections in a completely relaxed and livable way.

It is no secret to the woman of the house that when it comes to decorating, everyone gets into the act. No matter how

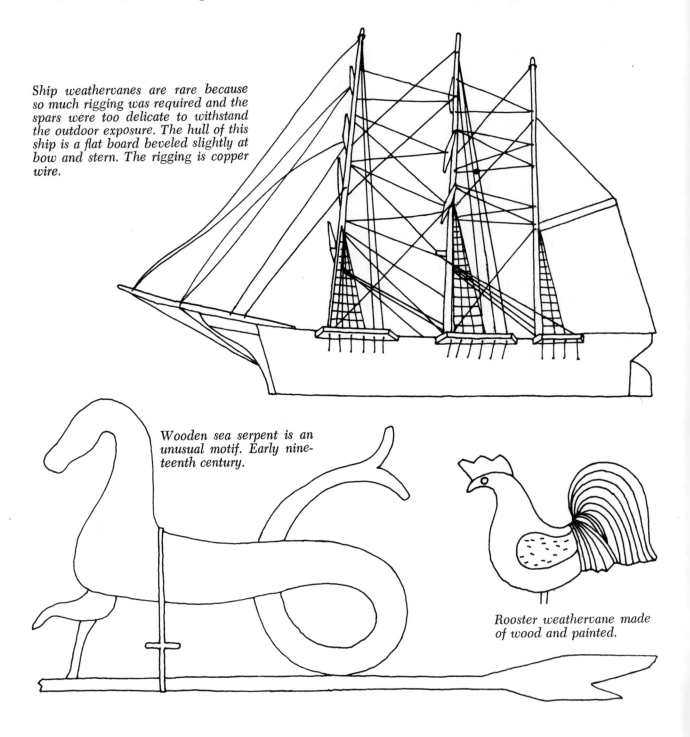

Ship weathervanes are rare because so much rigging was required and the spars were too delicate to withstand the outdoor exposure. The hull of this ship is a flat board beveled slightly at bow and stern. The rigging is copper wire.

Wooden sea serpent is an unusual motif. Early nineteenth century.

Rooster weathervane made of wood and painted.

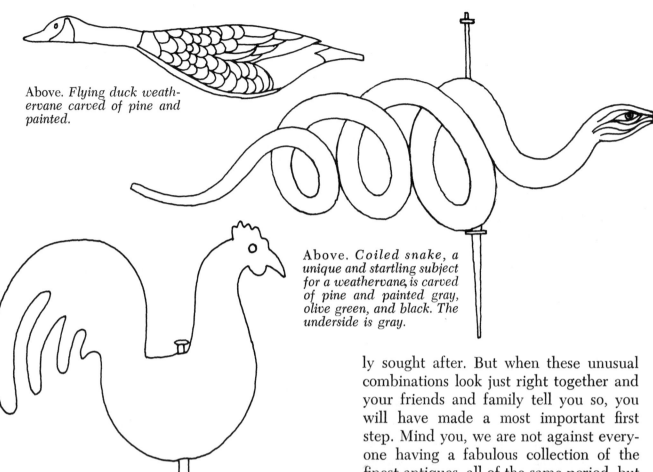

Above. *Flying duck weathervane carved of pine and painted.*

Above. *Coiled snake, a unique and startling subject for a weathervane, is carved of pine and painted gray, olive green, and black. The underside is gray.*

Rooster weathervane of wrought iron was made about 1800.

ly sought after. But when these unusual combinations look just right together and your friends and family tell you so, you will have made a most important first step. Mind you, we are not against everyone having a fabulous collection of the finest antiques, all of the same period, but we know that this is a difficult, expensive, and unusual proposition. Discussing it here would be no service to the majority of people, who have diverse collections—a few cherished pieces and some just for fun.

agreeable a husband is, he prefers things neat and blue. Fortunately, he usually prefers things worn and comfortable, too. It all tends to make it necessary for you, the decorator in charge, to work hard to be yourself, a young and contemporary idea much in vogue. You really must be fearless to combine antiques of classic form and high value with the later pieces of Americana that will not be important until you make them so. Antiques are known by the company they keep, and once they become popular, they are great-

Centaur weathervane was made of two sheets of copper, hammered into a convex form and soldered together. Bow and arrow and tail remain flat. Found near New Haven, Connecticut.

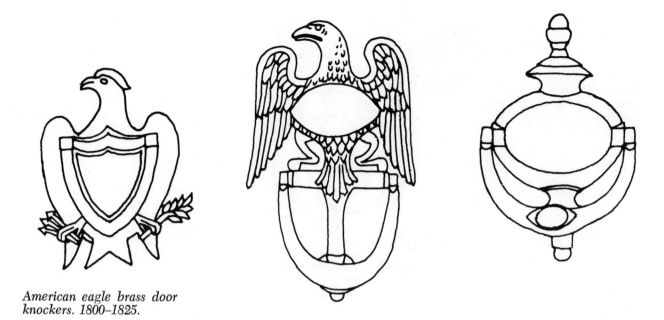

American eagle brass door knockers. 1800–1825.

What is most important to us is that perhaps we have motivated you to add to your collection and helped you to enjoy to the fullest the very things that prompted you to start collecting in the first place. What could be more pleasing than a late nineteenth century milk-glass bowl filled with nuts or grapes on a fine mahogany tilt-top table? Nothing makes dark wood look as lustrous and deep in color as white. A small piece of Victorian bric-a-brac, such as a cranberry glass pickle server, adds a bright bit of color and friendliness that a sterling silver bowl might not be able to lend. The silver may be richer and more expensive looking, but the warmth of the red might make the whole look brighter, gayer, and, most important of all, more fun to live with.

Painted and stenciled settee of the Hitchcock type, from the Philadelphia area. 1815–1830.

INDEX

Page numbers in boldface refer to illustrations.

238